COMPANION
TO
EARLY MIDDLE ENGLISH LITERATURE

edited by

N.H.G.E. VELDHOEN

and

H. AERTSEN

FREE UNIVERSITY PRESS

Amsterdam 1988

CIP-GEGEVENS KONINKLIJKE BIBLIOTHEEK, DEN HAAG

Companion

Companion to early Middle English literature / ed. by N.H.G.E. Veld-
hoen and H. Aertsen. - Amsterdam: Free University Press.
Met lit. opg.
ISBN 90-6256-632-4
SISO enge 852 UDC 820-024 NUGI 953
Trefw.: Middelengelse letterkunde.

PREFACE

The essays in this collection are introductions to a number of widely-read early Middle English texts, aimed at students who are coming to these texts with little experience of reading Middle English other than Chaucer. The purpose in each case is to stimulate a critical engagement by providing a literary approach and some historical context. Text-historical and linguistic analyses fall outside the scope of this book.

This collection of essays can be used alongside many anthologies of Middle English literature. References to texts are always to standard editions wherever possible.

This volume is a Dutch production: the authors and editors are all teaching, or have been teaching, at various universities in the Netherlands. Some of the contributions were originally written for a similar collection that has circulated for a few years as an internal publication of the English Department of the University of Leiden.

The present editors gratefully acknowledge the financial support of the "Malory *fonds*" of the Leiden Faculty of Letters which made the initial production possible. Our thanks are due also to Frans Grijzenhout of the Free University Press for his generous help and advice, to our colleague Cor Koster for his invaluable assistance with the Macintosh, and to Arno van Staalduine for his cheerful and patient typing out of the whole text.

University of Leiden
Free University, Amsterdam
July, 1988

N.H.G.E. Veldhoen
H. Aertsen

CONTENTS

THE MIDDLE ENGLISH LYRICS
AN INTRODUCTION

ALASDAIR A. MACDONALD
(University of Groningen)

A glance through any anthology of medieval literature suffices to reveal that, in those remote centuries, verse was a possible medium for many literary kinds for which the modern writer would naturally use prose (for example, sermons, histories, tales of adventure, philosophical disquisitions). Most of the poetry composed today is of the lyric sort, of which the more obvious characteristics are brevity, subjectivity, use of metaphor and symbol, registration and expression of strong emotions, and—as traditional formal features—stanzas, rhyme and regular rhythm. The difference between medieval and modern custom entrains two immediate consequences: first, we may find it difficult to consider the verse of lengthy romances and chronicles as, in a sense, real poetry; and second, when we encounter specimens of the medieval lyric we are liable to a pleasant shock of recognition which may be not quite warranted. While one may choose to see in the medieval lyric the beginning of a great tradition which continues to the present, one must be prepared also to make allowance for not a few points of difference.

Lyric poetry in English was one of the great innovations of the Middle Ages. But one naturally wonders first whether there are any connections with Old English verse. Although Anglo-Saxon poets were capable of expressing thoughts and feelings in memorable and rather special ('lyrical') language, they seem scarcely to have used the formal devices which later became so common. *Deor* and *Wulf and Eadwacer* might perhaps be said to use stanzas, and *The Riming Poem* and such pieces as the *Chronicle* poem on Alfred the Atheling (1036) show that rhyme was not unknown. Yet these very devices mark out such poems as exceptions in the Old English tradition, and Pearsall (1977:73; also, 70-74) has dismissed *The Riming Poem* as a "lunatic exercise". In some of the poems preserved in *The Anglo-Saxon Chronicle*, however, there is a trend towards unclassically regular two-stress rhythms and rhyme, which looks forward to such works as Laȝamon's *Brut* and *The Proverbs of Alfred*. The earliest Middle English lyrics for which music has survived, the songs of St Godric (d. 1170), show this kind of transitional writing, which seems to be moving towards stanza, rhyme and rhythm, but which is still organized on the basis of half-lines and employs alliteration, albeit of a rather attenuated type:

> Sainte Nicholas,   Godes druð,
> tymbre us faiere   scoone hus.
> At þi burðe,   at þi bare,
> Sainte Nicholas,   bring us wel þare.
>   (*MES*, 103)

(St Nicholas, beloved of God, prepare for us beautiful and lovely dwelling-places. Through the merits of thy birth and of thy death, bring us, St Nicholas, there in safety.)

By the thirteenth century, however, regular rhythm, rhyme and stanzas are firmly established, and alliteration, though it can still be important, is used in lyric verse not as a structural, but as a decorative feature.

The antecedents of the stanza-forms used in England in the Middle English lyric lie not in the native tradition, but in the Latin tradition of hymnody, which goes back to the Office hymns of St Ambrose (d. 397). There we find regularity of stanza and rhythm, and often rhyme as well. These Latin lyrics, well-known from constant use in church, exercised an enormous influence on the vernacular verse of Western Europe. Latin poems were themselves also influenced by vernacular song, and in all periods the religious and the secular lyrics remain closely in touch with one another (see Dronke, 1978:32-85). After the Norman Conquest, three languages were used for lyric verse in England: Latin, Anglo-Norman, and English. Not surprisingly, we find texts in which there appear, side by side, poems in all three tongues, and also lyrics in which there is a mixture of languages. In Bodleian MS Douce 139 there occurs the following brief definition of love:

Loue is a selkud wodenesse
Þat þe idel mon ledeth by wildernesse,
Þat þurstes of wilfulscipe and drinket sorwenesse
And with lomful sorwes menget his blithnesse.

(CB.XIII, 14-15)

(Love is an extraordinary madness, which leads the idle man through the wilderness, so that he thirsts after pleasure and drinks sorrow, and mingles his joy with continual griefs.)

These lines are accompanied by Latin and French versions of the same: *Amor est quedam mentis insania* etc., and *Amur est une pensee enragee* etc. With the texts of some poems—for example, *Eyns ne soy ke pleynte fu / Ar ne kuth ich sorghe non* ('Formerly I knew no sorrow'; *MES*, 110-111; *CB.XIII*, 10-13)—each of the English lines is given below its French counterpart (the French lines themselves follow musical notation): in this case the English is a reworking (*contrafactum*) of the French, and is to be sung to the same tune. However, behind the French words is a previous Latin poem of the type known as 'sequence', in which the stanzas, though they may vary the one from the other, nevertheless fall into two identically constructed halves. The English words of *Sumer is icumen in* (*MES*, 143; *CB.XIII*, 13), on the other hand, are found in BL MS Harley 978 *above* those in Latin, but, as Dobson and Harrison convincingly argue, this stems from the practical need to make the lines fill the allotted space, and does not imply prior composition in English (which, though possible, would be exceptional).

Whereas in the thirteenth century the exigencies of Latin musical forms frequently dictated the form of the resulting English poems, later in the medieval period lyrics were often purely literary creations, not based on pre-existing songs. Among the more celebrated specimens of this type of lyric may be mentioned the series of refrain poems from the Vernon MS, Bodleian MS Eng. poet. a.1 (*CB.XIV*, 125-208; Pearsall, 1977:140-143). Throughout the history of the Middle English lyric, the influence from both Latin and French models, musical and literary, sacred and secular, continued to be felt. With the eventual decline in the use of Anglo-Norman, however, the English lyrics gained in independence—although the Chaucerian poets were much obliged to Continental French models. For its part, the influence of Latin in the fourteenth to sixteenth centuries was no longer mainly at the level of form, but rather at that of content and expression.

The Middle English religious lyrics outnumber their secular counterparts by a ratio of about five to one. A number of reasons may be given for this. Since today we have only what has been written down, we can have little idea of what would have appealed to the taste of the illiterate majority of the population, should that have differed from the taste of the literate minority. To speak of medieval folksongs is very risky, while 'popular' song or verse could well have appealed (as today) to all classes of society and to all levels of education. Another factor is that of chance survival: we have no sure grounds for assuming that the extant remains are truly representative of the entire corpus of lyrics. Furthermore, we are at the mercy of the copyists. Most English lyrics are found in manuscripts linked with monasteries or other religious houses, and we may surmise that the scribes and authors were monks, priests, friars, or, at the least, clerics in minor orders. Although it would be rash to assume that the tastes of these men were necessarily narrow, it is obvious that religious material, which was officially approved, would stand the best chance of being preserved. Many secular lyrics, indeed, are known only from chance scribblings in the margins of more 'respectable' works.

Interpretation and critical appreciation of the Middle English lyrics makes desirable our knowing something about the identity of the authors, the occasions for which the poems were composed, the opportunities for performance, the functions the poems were intended to have, and the rhetorical means by which these functions were effected. It is, of course, possible to dispense with these preparatives, and to approach the poems 'blind'. With unfamiliar art forms, however, there is little chance that an immediate response—be it ever so sincerely or strongly felt—will be very helpful. Moreover, the modern reader may have to disabuse himself of hand-me-down critical assumptions—such as a tendency to generalise about 'medievalism' and to find it romantic, or to consider the lyrics as evincing charming naivety, rugged simplicity, primitive purity, of any combination thereof. The critic may indeed find certain lyrics charming, or simple, or primitive, but his finding will take its value from the appreciation of the context in which the poems belong. This problem of critical interference bedevils the study of the lyrics more than that of other medieval works or genres because of the treacherous continuity in the composition of the lyrics, and because it has sometimes been supposed that a medieval lyric can be adequately approached as if it had been composed yesterday. Edith Sitwell (1972:245) described *Maid in the moor lay* (*MES*, 188-189) as a 'miracle of poetry': the phrase perhaps suggests more about her conception of poetry than it illuminates the medieval work itself.

The biographical approach is not of much help to the student of Middle English lyrics, since so little is known about even those few poets whose names are recorded. The obscurity does not mean, however, that the poems were the spontaneous or long-evolved creations of an anonymous 'folk'. Rather, the obscurity is the result of accidental losses of information, on the one hand, and, on the other, the fact that, from the outset, the lyrics were intended for general use and were not conceived as the expression of the unique thoughts and experiences of particular individuals, recollected in conditions of more or less tranquillity. It is possible, nonetheless, to say something about the authors' background and the cultural milieu in which they were working. The very use of the English language suggests that the intended audience was the ordinary people: the priests had their Latin, and the Court (until the fifteenth century) its French. The religious lyrics can be seen as giving poetic expression to the tasks of quickening and propagating the faith, and their survival is a measure of their success. The secular lyrics—of which the great majority would also be the work of clerics—similarly reach out to please their English-speaking audience.

It is especially (though not exclusively) the Franciscan friars who are associated with the religious lyrics: for example, Thomas of Hales (c. 1275), William Herebert (d. 1333), John Grimestone (c. 1372), James Ryman (late fifteenth century). Unlike the monks, the friars travelled widely among the people, frequently preached in the open air at preaching-crosses, and were even regarded as competitors by the parish priests. In their sermons they often made use of vernacular verse, and several of the manuscripts which preserve Middle English lyrics are, in fact, anthologies assembled by friars (Pearsall, 1977:132-40; Wenzel, 1978:61-132; Wilson, 1973:vii-xvi). The role of the Franciscans in the religious lyric is also borne out by the manuscripts, which show many shared items. This permits one to conclude that the best lyrics must have been circulated by the friars in their travels. Of all types of religious lyric the most popular was indubitably the carol, and R.L. Greene has discussed the important part played by the Franciscans in the composition, transcription and dissemination of such pieces (1977:cl-clvii).In one lyric (not a carol) in Bodleian MS Digby 2 (*CB.XIII*, 126) we find the line, *Frer menur I wil me make*: this is—one must assume—the putative resolution of one who had already joined the order. In fact, in the history of the Middle English lyrics one can hardly overemphasize the contribution made by the friars.

The church liturgy was, of course, conducted in Latin, but there were plenty opportunities for the extraliturgical use of religious lyrics: for example, in the course of sermons, during processions, during banquets, in the speeches of characters in religious dramas, and in optional musical fragments, such as the substitution of vernacular pieces for the often sung phrase, *Benedicamus domino*. Other lyrics would have been used in the private devotions of individuals. Many so-called lyrics are humble versifications of the *Pater Noster*, *Ave Maria* or *Credo*, with few literary pretensions. Other lyrics—listing such things as the joys and sorrows (five, seven, or fifteen) of Our Lady, or the various headings under which sins might be confessed (the five wits, the seven deadly sins, the seven deeds of corporal and spiritual mercy, the seven sacraments, the ten commandments, the twelve articles of faith, etc.)—doubtless owed their popularity to their mnemonic usefulness. Again, the subject-matter of many religious lyrics may be connected with the festivals of the church year (for example, the Annunciation, Nativity, Passion and Resurrection), and it is important to take this context into account. While it would be naive to suppose that medieval congregations did not understand what regular iteration had made familiar to them in the Latin of the church services, they would presumably respond with greater immediacy to devotional texts in their own language, and which were not restricted to use in church. It is no accident that the greatly increased composition of religious lyrics in the fourteenth, fifteenth and early sixteenth centuries coincides with the growth of devotions with a wide appeal (for example, to the Holy Name, the Five Wounds, the Rosary), and with the use in manuscript and printed Books of Hours of iconographic figures (for example, the *imago pietatis*, Christ displaying the wounds of the Crucifixion; the *arma Christi*, the instruments of the Passion; the mass of St Gregory, illustrating the miraculous power of the Eucharist) which could be 'imprinted' on the imagination, in order to stimulate meditation. The later Middle Ages, furthermore, witnessed a remarkable development of Marian devotion, and this is clearly reflected in the enthusiasm for lyrics on this theme (Woolf, 1968:274-308, 389-91; Gray, 1972:18-30). Yet another factor to be borne in mind is that the religious lyrics in the case of versifications of approved prayer texts were often associated with indulgences: this was a sure passport to popularity in the eschatologically-minded later Middle Ages. For example, the lyric, *Haill Mary, quhais concepcioun*, is a rendering of the Latin verses, *Ave cuius concepcio*, which was one of the commonest items in Books of Hours; this prayer carried an indulgence from Pope Sixtus IV, in the terms of which the length of time spent in Purgatory by the soul of the person devoutly saying the prayer was reduced by 11000 years (Bennett, 1955:xx-xxi). An awareness of the devotional practices of medieval society thus greatly helps one to understand why religious lyrics were written, and what purposes they were designed to serve.

Two brief illustrations may be given of the continuing appeal, but also the textual problems, of the Middle English lyrics. The thirteenth-century poem *Of on þat is so fayr and briʒt*, from BL MS Egerton 613 (*CB.XIII*, 26-27), was rearranged to make the later lyric *A lady þat was so feyre & briʒt* (Bodleian MS Ashmole 1393; fifteenth century; *CB.XV*, 34-35). Both mingle short lines of English with lines consisting of familiar Latin religious tags. The earlier poem has forty-five lines, in nine-line stanzas. In the later poem these are trimmed to twenty-eight lines in four-line stanzas (and survive with music). Though a great deal is shared between the two poems, there is a perceptible change in emphasis. Whereas in the first version we find a loving wonderment at Mary's role in the miraculous scheme of salvation, in the second there is a sharper focus on the honour which she thereby deserves. The later version ends thus:

> Of all wymmen þu berist þe price,
> mater generosa,
> Grawnt vs all paradys,
> virgo gloriosa.
> (*CB.XV*, 35)

This is a revision of a pair of lines which appear near the middle of the earlier version, but the use of the lines as conclusion quite changes the impact. As a result of such modifications a tighter, more effective poem has been produced.

The second example is provided by the celebrated fifteenth-century *I syng of a myden* (i.e. maiden; *CB.XV*, 119), which uses lines from the poem *Nu þis fules singet* (*CBX.III*, 55):

> I syng of a myden   þat is makeles,
> kyng of alle kynges   to here sone che ches.
> he cam also stylle   þer his moder was
> as dew in aprylle,   þat fallyt on þe gras.
> he cam also stylle   to his moderes bowr
> as dew in aprille,   þat fallyt on þe flour.
> he cam also stylle   þer his moder lay
> as dew in aprille,   þat fallyt on þe spray.
> moder & mayden was neuer non but che --
> wel may swych a lady godes moder be.
> (CB.XV, 119)

(I sing of a maiden, peerless, without stain: she chose the king of all kings as her son. He came so softly where his mother was, like dew in April falling on the grass. He came so softly to his mother's chamber, like dew in April falling on the flower. He came so softly where his mother lay, like dew in April falling on the blossom. None but she was ever mother and maiden: such a lady can truly be the Mother of God.)

The scriptural basis of the two poems is the account of the Annunciation in St Luke's gospel (i, 26-38), and also the text of Isaiah (xiv, 8) which uses the image of dew as a figuration of the divine grace which falls on the earth. It is small wonder that the latter text is much quoted in the liturgy during the period of Advent, just before the celebration of the birth of Christ. The earlier poem shows the scriptural narrative recast into fairly straightforward verse, whereas the later one shows a real poetic power which derives from the total concentration on the central metaphor of dew, with its obvious connotations of beauty, moisture, purity and fertility, together with the slow disclosure of the initial mystery as one comes gradually to realise the identity of the maiden. *Nu þis fules singet* retells the paradox; *I syng of a myden* enacts it. The success of the later poem has nothing to do with novelty of thought, but everything to do with artistic control over expression.

Wen þe turuf is þi tuur (*CB.XIII*, 54) is a lyric which clearly shows the need for criticism of medieval poetry to begin with an appreciation of the medieval context—in this case the literature of courtly love:

Wen þe turuf is þi tuur,
& þi put is þi bour,
þi wel & þi wite þrote
ssulen wormes to note.
Wat helpit þe þenne
al þe worilde wnne?

(*CB.XIII*, 54)

(When the turf is your tower and your grave your bedchamber, your skin and your white throat shall be food for worms. What will it help you then, all the profit of the world?)

The method of the poet here is to contrast sharply the 'tower' (of the castle of love, of safety in the pride of life) and the 'bower' (of intimate erotic and social intercourse) with the grim physical reality of the 'turf' and 'pit' (of the grave). Love and death, transience and eternity, light and darkness, warmth and chill, the delights of the human imagination and the ineluctable conditions of human existence—these are the antinomies which the poem evokes, and the use of alliteration forces one to consider both terms of the stark contrasts. The brevity of the poem allows the reader no escape from the intended *frisson*: he must recognise that the foundations of his behaviour and values are as shadows in the light of eternal verities. It is good that the lyric ends with the challenge of the rhetorical question. The unspoken answer is clear, though men may choose to forget it: to spell it out would be unnecessary, and poetically disastrous. In this lyric the author's artistic discretion brilliantly succeeds in communicating his message, yet, after this is understood in terms of the medieval vision of life, we can see that the poem has also achieved a power to affect which is universal. As with many other early Middle English lyrics, one of the chief poetic successes of this piece (which is actually a translation from Latin) is a laconic expression which makes the lines seem pregnant with meaning. At its best it is an art of concentration.

The very important BL MS Harley 2253 bears out most of what has been said above. It contains prose and verse, lyrics and longer poems, Latin, French and English. One or two lyrics, indeed, use all three languages—as in this stanza, which concludes a macaronic lyric presumably composed by a student-cleric at the University of Paris:

> Scripsi hec carmina in tabulis;
> mon ostel est en mi la vile de Paris;
> may y sugge namore, so wel me is;
> ȝef hi deȝe for loue of hire, duel hit ys.

(HL, 55)

(I have written these verses in my will; my lodging is in the middle of the city of Paris; I can say no more, so great is my good fortune; if I die for love of her, it will be a grievous sorrow.)

The manuscript, taken as a whole, clearly reflects the learned tastes of the compilers, and the poem just quoted is evidently the work of a thirteenth-century 'university wit'. Such people would be quite likely to import into English poetry French (Provençal and Northern) literary fashions, such as, within the general European craze for courtly love, the *reverdie* (a song of Spring), the *chanson d'aventure* (a light-hearted narrative of love), and the *pastourelle* (a variant of the previous, involving a knight and a female social inferior, often in a woodland setting).

The variety of dialect features displayed by the Harley lyrics shows that many of them originated outside the West Midlands, where they were collected by some churchman, perhaps in Leominster, near Hereford. The special importance of this Harley text lies in the number of delightful secular lyrics which it preserves, although these are only a small proportion of the total contents of the manuscript. If one remembers the even more celebrated medieval collection, the *Carmina Burana*, one will not be surprised that love poems so appealed in ecclesiastical circles. One lyric, *My de þ y loue* (*CB.XIII*, 152-154; *HL*, 62-63), shows a clerical lover at work, charming his victim into a surrender which is far from undesired; the testimony of the Wife of Bath confirms the appeal of such *glosing* (Chaucer *WB* 509).

Another Harley poem, *Mosti ryden by Rybbesdale* (*HL*,37-39), consists mainly of an itemised list of the lady's attractions, and there is a charming physicality (somewhat in the manner of Robert Herrick) in the lines. This allows of easy visualisation: one will remember the grey eyes, the arching brows, the whalebone-white teeth, the skin whiter than

morning-fresh milk. The poet fantasises about riding through Ribbles-
dale (in Lancashire) to choose one of the 'wilde wymmen', but the lady of
his choice is praised in courtly terms. Her red lips are ideal *romaunz
forte rede*, and the climax of the poem wittily plays on the conjunction of
a heavenly and earthly paradise:

> He myhte sayen þat Crist hym seȝe
> þat myhte nyhtes neh hyre leȝe,
>   heuene ne heuede here.
>
> (*HL*, 39)

(He could say that Christ was watching over him; he who could lie at night beside her would be enjoying heaven here.)

The lady's breasts are *as apples tuo of Parays*, and the poet would choose
to watch for her coming, rather than *beon pope ant ryde in Rome*. The
hyperbolical nature of many of the compliments contained in the poem is
typical of medieval clerical wit.

The tone and expression of a lyric are not predetermined by the
subject-matter, although they will naturally be influenced by it. There are
many things to say about love and many ways of saying them, and this
variety applies no less to religious subjects. What counts is the coordina-
tion of form—whether song, narrative, prayer, exposition, invective,
mnemonic or meditation—with the affective purpose intended. The early
lyric, *Nou goth sonne vnder wod* (*CB.XIII*, 1), found with the Passion
meditation for sext (Mary's commission to St John) in the *Speculum
Ecclesiae* of St Edmund of Abingdon (d. 1240), and William Dunbar's
Amang thir freiris, within ane cloister (late fifteenth/early sixteenth
century) are both personal meditations on the Passion, yet, whereas the
former is justly celebrated for its tremendous understatement, the latter
contains a brutally pictorial narrative of the sufferings of Christ,
followed by an account in allegorical terms of the effect upon the medi-
tator (in Kinsley, 1979:7-11). The differences between the two poems are
enormous; yet, though the juxtaposition reveals two radically different
conceptions of religious lyric poetry, the underlying function of the
lyrics is similar. One could likewise oppose the simple, fourteenth-
century lyric from the school of Richard Rolle, *Lo! lemman swete, now
may þou se* (*CB.XIV*, 94), with the early sixteenth-century lyric, *O man*

remember and prent in to þi thocht, of William Stewart (*Bannatyne MS,* ii.90-95). In each poem, Christ asks man to remember what He has suffered for him. The first concludes with all the tenderness of divine love:

> And, swete lemman, forget þow noght
> þat I þi lufe sa dere haue boght,
>   And I aske þe noght elles.
>   (*CB.XIV*, 94)

(And forget not, sweet loved-one, that I so dearly have bought your love, and I ask nothing else from you.)

The second, however, is the work of a stern moralist, and the refrain which Stewart puts into the mouth of Christ has a distinctly threatening ring to it: *Amend thy mis, this plaig sall pas the fra* ('reform your sinful life, and this plague shall leave you'). For most types of lyrics, sacred and secular, one could probably find a commensurately wide range of expressive possibilities.

The period of the medieval English lyric extends from the twelfth to the early sixteenth centuries, and an evolution along the way is only to be expected. Among the qualities of the early Middle English lyric may be remarked an engaging freshness in the love poems and a dense brevity in the religious poems. In later centuries one sees a greater use of rhetorical colours, a growing elaboration of stanza forms, an increasing love of latinate vocabulary (aureate terms), and a tendency for the lyrics to discard the anonymity of their predecessors. Yet these trends were not exclusive, and there are masterly lyrics and carols in the simple style in the fifteenth century. The Middle English lyric is not a monolithic phenomenon, but a richly diverse art form which was continually developing. Though many of these poems achieve a universality of appeal which may speak to us across the centuries, they all benefit from a critical approach which tries to see them against the cultural background on which they drew and of which they are an expression.

ABBREVIATED TITLES

Bannatyne MS.:: The Bannatyne MS. Ed. W. Tod Ritchie. 4 Vols. Scottish Text Society. Edinburgh and London. 1928-34.
CB.XIII :: *English Lyrics of the Thirteenth Century*. Ed. C. Brown. Oxford: O.U.P. 1932.
CB.XIV :: *Religious Lyrics of the Fourteenth Century*. Ed. C. Brown. 2nd ed. rev. G.V. Smithers. Oxford: O.U.P. 1957.
CB.XV :: *Religious Lyrics of the Fifteenth Century*. Ed. C. Brown. Oxford: O.U.P. 1939.
Chaucer *WB*. In: *The Works of Geoffrey Chaucer*. Ed. F.N. Robinson. 2nd ed. Boston, Mass.: Houghton Mifflin [Cambridge, Mass.: Riverside Press], and London: O.U.P. 1957. (1st ed., 1933.)
HL :: *The Harley Lyrics*. Ed. G.L. Brook. 4th ed. Manchester: Manchester U.P. 1968.
MES :: *Medieval English Songs*. Ed. E.J. Dobson and F.Ll. Harrison. London: Faber and Faber.1979.

OTHER REFERENCES

Bennett, J.A.W. (ed.) (1955). *Devotional Pieces in Verse and Prose*. Scottish Text Society. Edinburgh and London.
Dronke, P. (1978). *The Medieval Lyric*. 2nd ed. London: Hutchinson.
Gray, D. (1972). *Themes and Images in the Medieval English Religious Lyric*. London: Routledge and Kegan Paul.
Greene, R.L. (1977). *The Early English Carols*. 2nd ed. Oxford: O.U.P.
Kinsley, J. (ed.) (1979). *The Poems of William Dunbar*. Oxford: O.U.P.
Pearsall, D. (1977). *Old and Middle English Poetry*. London: Routledge and Kegan Paul.
Sitwell, E. (1972). *A Poet's Notebook*. Westport, Conn.: Greenwood (1st publ. London: Macmillan 1943).
Wenzel, S. (1978). *Verses in Sermons*. Cambridge, Mass.: Harvard U.P.
Wilson, E. (ed.) (1973). *A Descriptive Index of the English Lyrics in John of Grimestone's Preaching Book*. Medium Ævum Monographs, N.S. II. Oxford.
Woolf, R. (1968). *The English Religious Lyric in the Middle Ages*. Oxford: O.U.P..

ST KENELM AND THE LEGENDS OF THE ENGLISH SAINTS IN THE *SOUTH ENGLISH LEGENDARY*

RENEE HAMELINCK
(Utrecht)

When the *South English Legendary* (*SEL*) was composed in the Worcester area at the end of the thirteenth century, collections of saints' legends existed in various countries and in different languages. They were based on a collection of saints' legends in Latin, the *Legenda Aurea*. However, "national saints tended to become appended to or inserted into *LgA* [*Legenda Aurea*] manuscripts in different European countries" (Görlach, 1973:23). Almost a fifth of the legends assembled in the *SEL* are about English saints. Because of the compiler's decision to order the legends according to the distribution of the saints' feastdays over the year, the legends about the English saints are scattered over the entire work. As a result, the underlying unity of the legends does not immediately become clear, but a closer examination of the material reveals that the compiler has apparently selected the legends to serve specific purposes.

Together the legends relate the history of the English church from the time when Christianity was first brought to England by St Augustine up to the thirteenth century when the *SEL* was composed. The most recently canonized saint in the collection is Edmund Rich, Archbishop of Canterbury, whose canonization took place some fifty years before the collection was compiled. The development of the English church as related in the legends shows how, after a period of prosperity under the Anglo-Saxon kings, its position becomes increasingly weakened after the Norman kings came to power. When St Augustine is sent to England on a mission to convert the people, he expects a hostile reception. Contrary to his expectations, the heathen King Ethelbert, although not willing to accept the new religion before thoroughly examining it, receives the missionary well and gives him ample freedom to carry out his preaching activities. When he has come to the conclusion that the new religion is a good one, he full-heartedly accepts it. Thus a period of prosperity for the Christian church under the Anglo-Saxon kings commences. The kings support the church and encourage its bishops in the spreading of the new faith throughout the country.

The relationship between the kings and the church is one of the main points of interest in the legends about the English saints. Some of the Anglo-Saxon kings take the church's welfare so much to heart that they themselves become saints, as is the case with the kings Oswald, Edward the Elder and Edward the Confessor. When the king and the church support each other, prosperity comes to the people of the country. This can be seen in the legend of St Edward the Elder, who relies heavily upon the advice of his bishop Dunstan, who

> ... was glad of him . and al is lond also
> Of such king þat was hore louerd . þat fonde so wel to do
> God pais þer was in Engelond . & loue & ioye inou
> Richesse and al oþer god . for elles it were wou
> For wanne þe heued haþ Godes grace . & loueþ alle gode
> Wonder hit were bote al his . þe betere bistode
> *Edward the Elder*, 23-28 [1]

(... was pleased with him, and so was his whole country with such a king as their lord was, who tried to do so well. There was great peace in England, and plenty of love and joy, wealth and all other goods, because otherwise it would be a sad truth. For when the head has God's grace, and loves all goodness, it would be strange if all his [people] did not prosper the better.)

The prosperity of England depends directly upon the king, who can make his country prosper by listening to the advice of his ecclesiastical counsellors, and thus deserve God's grace. When the king acts against God's wish, it is not only the church, but the entire country which suffers as a result. When King Ethelred comes to the throne after murdering his stepbrother King Edward, Bishop Dunstan predicts great misery which will not only affect the king but also

> ... þe lond folk of Engelond . þat no gult nabbeþ þerto
> For more wrechede & sorwe . þer comeþ bi þine daye
> Into Engelond uor þulke sunne . þan me euere iseye
> *Edward the Elder*, 110-112

---

[1] All quotations are from the text edition by D'Evelyn and Mill (1956-59).

(... the people of England, who have no guilt in it. For greater misery and sorrow will come in your time to England because of that sin, than has ever been seen.)

It is not until Ethelred's son, Edward the Confessor, becomes king that England prospers again.

In the legends about the English saints, the early English period is looked back upon with nostalgia. The time when the head of state and the church are supporting each other comes to an end with the death of the last Anglo-Saxon king, Edward the Confessor. The tragedy which affects the country is described in the legend of St Wulfstan.

Four ȝer he [Wulfstan] hadde bissop ibe[o] . & noȝt follich fyue
To seint Edward þe holy king . wende out of þis liue
To gret ruþe to al Engelonde . so weilawei þe stonde
For strange men þer come suþþe . & broȝte Engelond to gronde

Wulfstan, 57-60

(He had been bishop for four years, and not fully five, when Saint Edward, the holy king, departed from this life, which was a cause of great sorrow to all England, alas the time! For foreign men came afterwards, and brought England to ruin.)

The decline of the English church starts with the arrival of William the Conqueror, who brought England under Norman and feudal rule. From then on the legends of the English saints no longer describe a state of harmony between the ruler and the church, but the saints meet growing opposition in their plans and actions for the benefit of the church. While the earlier legends show that, in general, the Anglo-Saxon kings were more than willing to listen to their bishops' advice, the Norman kings, for their part, were not, resenting the bishops' opinions where these differed from their own, and fearing encroachment upon the power of the king. But the conflict is not only one between secular ruler and saint: it is a conflict between old values and new, which were forced upon the English by the invaders. The foreign rulers are definitely not accepted as the rightful kings of England, as is stated in unambiguous terms in the legend of St Wulfstan in the Ashmole MS. The battle between Harold and William the Conqueror brings the Norman king victory and Harold

... was byneþe ibroȝt . & ouercome attelaste
& ibroȝt to gronde & alle his . & al engelond also
Ibrouȝt in strange menne hond . þat lute riȝt hadde þerto
þat neuer eft hit ne com aȝen . to riȝt heires non
Vnkunde heires ȝut hi beþ . oure kynges euerichon

Wulfstan, 86-90

(... was brought down, and was overcome at last, and he and all his men per-
ished, and also all of England was brought into strange men's hands, who had
little right to it. So that it was never afterwards restored to any rightful heir.
They are still unrightful heirs, each one of our kings.)

The crisis between worldly ruler and saint reaches its climax in the
conflict between Archbishop Thomas Becket and King Henry II. Due to
the compiler's decision to order the legends according to the distribution
of the saints' feastdays over the year, the legend of Thomas Becket, whose
festival was on 29th December, is the last one of the collection, and was
clearly intended to be its highlight. The conflicts between the archbishop
and the king over the rights of the church are described in great detail.
Whereas the king wants Becket's complete submission to his wishes, the
archbishop thinks that Henry is trying to curtail the power of the church
and he is only willing to obey the king's commands when they do not
endanger the church's power. As the tension between the two men
mounts, the only solution to the problem seems to be Becket's death. To
defend the church's rights the saint is willing to suffer martyrdom:

Icham for Holy Churche riȝte . iredy þane deþ auonge
Biddeþ for me for Godes loue . and for Holy Churche also
þat geþ almest nou to gronde . bote God nyme ȝeme þertwo

Thomas Becket, 1982-1984

(I am ready then to receive death for the right of the Holy Church. Pray for me
for God's love and also for the Holy Church which is now almost destroyed,
unless God takes heed of it.)

When Henry's knights murder Becket on the consecrated ground of
Canterbury Cathedral, the tragic climax in the history of the English

church has been reached. A choice has been made in favour of secular power and against the church.

But Becket is more than a representative of the church: his opposition to the unjust plans of the king and his stubbornness in defending his rights symbolize a growing self-awareness among the English people who are becoming increasingly discontented with the foreign rulers and desire to have the good times under the Anglo-Saxon kings restored.

Among the legends about the English saints in the *SEL* the legend of Saint Kenelm takes up an interesting position. The legend relates how Kenelm succeeds his father to the throne of Mercia when he is only seven years old. His sister Quendride resents his power and plans to have her brother murdered. It is Kenelm's guardian Askebert who performs the foul act by decapitating the boy and hiding his body in the forest. When people have forgotten about Kenelm, a cow makes it its habit to sleep on the spot where the king is buried. Although the animal's behaviour is believed to have a miraculous meaning, this is not understood until God reveals in a message from Heaven to the Pope in Rome the place where Kenelm's body lies hidden. Soon the body is discovered, and the young king is buried beside his father in Winchcombe, whereas Quendride receives her just punishment when she is dragged out of town and her body is thrown into a ditch.

Although Kenelm is venerated as a martyr in the *SEL*, he did not suffer death because of his faith, and therefore cannot strictly be called a martyr. His case is not unique: the *SEL* also includes King Edward in its list of martyrs, although this king was murdered over a matter of succession to the throne, and not as a result of his religious opinions. The events described in Edward's legend correspond with the historical facts, whereas there is no doubt that the story of Kenelm's life and death does not correspond with what is known about him. According to the most important historical document of the Anglo-Saxon period, *the Anglo-Saxon Chronicle*, Kenelm's father, King Kenulf, was succeeded by his brother Cedwulf. Kenelm is not mentioned at all in the *Chronicle*, and the only historical evidence which exists of him is a number of documents which he signed as "Cynhelm princeps" or "Cynhelm dux" between 803 and 811, when he must have been about fourteen years old. This means that Kenelm was at least twenty-four when his father died in 819, and not a boy of seven as is stated in the legend.[2] Little historical value can be attached to the description of Quendride, Kenelm's wicked sister, either. As it is known that she was an abbess during her lifetime, there seems to be no reason to assume that she wanted to murder her brother. It is therefore likely that the characters of the two leading persons in the legend, Kenelm and Quendride, were adapted to suit their roles: a child who is martyred is more pathetic than an adult, and Quendride has to oppose this child with full wickedness so that his virtue is demonstrated more clearly.

One of the reasons justifying the inclusion of Kenelm's legend in the *SEL* is the saint's immense popularity in the south of England, where the *SEL* was compiled. It is even likely that people had begun to worship Kenelm as a saint long before he was officially canonized. Quite frequently a saint was canonized under pressure of the popularity he enjoyed among the common people (De Grijs, 1983:18). The centre of Kenelm's veneration was in Winchcombe, and it was there that many people assembled on his feastday on 17th July. In his *De Gestis Regum Anglorum* William of Malmesbury claims that nowhere in England did so many people gather as on Kenelm's Feastday, although it must be admitted that a large crowd might also have been attracted by the big annual market which was held in Winchcombe on the same day (see Von Antropoff, 1956:29-30). There is no doubt, however, that Kenelm was a particularly popular saint among the common people, and it is especially at this audience that the legend of the saint in the *SEL* is directed.

The second reason why Kenelm's legend was included in the collection is that it fits in with the sentiments expressed in the group of legends about the English saints, as will become evident when the legend is discussed in more detail.

The story opens with a long description of Anglo-Saxon England at the time of Kenelm. It describes the state of England before the invasions, the 'pure kingdom'. The purpose of the long description, which takes up about one-sixth of the total length of the legend, is twofold. Firstly it is meant to demonstrate that Mercia was the most powerful of the five kingdoms, which explains why Kenelm's sister is envious of her brother's wealth when he becomes king. It is Quendride's envy which causes

---

[2] For a more detailed description of the historical facts about Kenelm, see Von Antropoff, 1956:23-25.

Kenelm's tragic death and triggers off the action in the narrative. The description is also meant to remind the audience of the history of the country—a history they could be proud of. The undertone of nationalistic pride accords with that found in the other legends of English saints and fits in with the policy of King Edward I, who made a conscious effort to emphasize his Anglo-Saxon roots. Named after the last great Anglo-Saxon king, Edward the Confessor, Edward I suppressed his Norman descent and sought to strengthen his grip on the English throne by stressing his Anglo-Saxon lineage, and by stimulating a new nationalistic feeling in his subjects.

Whereas the description of the Anglo-Saxon kingdoms based on historical truth, the description of Kenelm and Quendride was not, as has been suggested above. All through the legend Kenelm's youth is emphasized, and it is shown how an innocent child falls victim to the wicked intentions of the adults surrounding him. Kenelm's innocence causes God's grace to rest upon him. When the child is not affected by the poison which Quendride administers to him in her first attempt to dispose of her brother, it is explained to the audience that God will not allow Kenelm to be martyred so easily. It becomes clear that the child has to fulfil a special role in the Divine Plan. There is no indication that Kenelm himself is aware of his special position in God's plan—he remains ignorant of the harm which his sister tried to conflict upon him.

In many legends God's working a miracle for the saint creates an emotional distance between the saint and the audience. The saint no longer moves on the same level as other people: he has transcended that and has grown in spiritual posture. This alienation has consciously been avoided in *St Kenelm* by emphasizing the saint's ignorance of God's design and by the fact that he is only a child. The frequent repetition of the word "child" serves to keep Kenelm on a level with the audience, who remain emotionally involved with him.

The same innocence speaks from Kenelm's inability to interpret the dream he has about the ash-tree. He dreams how his dearest friend cuts down the tree with the intention of killing Kenelm who was sitting on one of its boughs. When the tree falls, Kenelm changes into a white dove and flies to Heaven. From a narrative point of view, the recounting of the dream heightens the suspense in the story: as Kenelm's nurse explains to the boy, the dream foreshadows his death. But the dream is also symbolic of God's grace resting upon the young king: the white dove which flies to Heaven symbolizes Kenelm's soul which will be taken up into the glory of Heaven. The dove is also a symbol of hope. Although Kenelm may be overcome by evil when his guardian murders him, his death will not remain unavenged, and is indeed necessary to reveal God's power, which is the people's hope.

When the people have forgotten about Kenelm after he has been murdered, it is *a dombe best wiþoute witte* (l.220: 'a dumb animal without intelligence') which is chosen as the instrument for God's miracle. The cow always returns to the spot where the king's body lies hidden. It does not eat, but still produces more milk every day, which makes the composer exclaim:

> Wo so hadde such kun inowe . he nere noʒt bymene
> þei is larder were nei do . and is somer lese lene
>
> *St Kenelm* 235-236

> Who possessed enough of such cows need not be pitied, even if his provision chamber were almost empty, and his summer pasture lean.)

This observation, which might well have been a later addition to the text by the compiler, clearly wants to evoke a direct response from the audience, who, judging from the nature of the remark, cannot have been an upper class one. Most of the legends in the *SEL* aim at a lower class audience; it is mainly for them that the saints work their miracles.

The miracle of the cow also leads to another miracle, for although the common people recognize the cow's behaviour as miraculous, they cannot fully interpret its meaning. Although God's miracles can be seen by all men, the church is needed to explain them for them. In the legend of Kenelm, it is God Himself who explains the miracle to His people. This happens when God sends a *writ* from Heaven to the Pope in Rome, which states:

> In Clent Coubach Kenelm kinges bern
> Liþ vnder a þorn heued bireued
>
> *St Kenelm* 267-268

> (In Cowbach in Clent lies Kenelm, the king's son, under a thorn-tree, deprived of his head.)

The message provides the information necessary to understand the cow's behaviour. This miracle is the highlight of the legend, and it explains why *St Kenelm* takes up a key position among the legends of the English saints in the *SEL*. The letter with God's explanation comes straight from Heaven and is directed to the English people, which is made clear by the fact that it is written in English. The Pope cannot understand the divine message, but the English people can! Kenelm's martyrdom, then, was necessary for God to reveal the special place which the English have in His divine plan. It is no wonder that this writing is stated to be the most wonderful relic: *Wat noblore relike miȝte be[o] . i necan noȝt vnderstonde* (l.274: 'I cannot perceive what more splendid relic there could be').

The miracle links the different layers of the narrative. In the story proper it leads to the discovery of the body and the restoring of justice. When Kenelm's body is carried back to the town of Winchcombe, Quendride loses her power to inflict harm upon others. When she tries to curse her brother's corpse, the curse falls upon herself and her eyes fall out. Thus she is punished for her misdeeds. Balance is restored when she is dragged out of town and thrown into a ditch and dies a shameful death, whereas Kenelm's remains are carried into Winchcombe in triumph and are enshrined in the abbey.

The miracle also demonstrates that God uses His saints as an instrument to reveal His love for the people. The virtuous Anglo-Saxon boy-king Kenelm is proof of this. Hence the legend of Kenelm takes the audience back to the good Anglo-Saxon times when God's love was expressed so openly, and for everyone to see. The *SEL* regrets that those times were over with the coming of the Norman rulers, whose desire for absolute power inflicts harm upon the church and makes it difficult for the people to discover God's intentions. All that is left of the miracles worked for the English people in the old times are the saints' relics and the places where the miracles were worked for the saints. Such a place is the well which springs to quench the thirst of the people who are carrying Kenelm's body back from the forest to Winchcombe. The well still existed when the legend was composed, and it is said that

Wel faire it is iheled nou . wiþ freo ston as riȝt is
Iredi ech mon to drinke of . þat comeþ þeruorþ iwis

þe monkes su þ þe of Winchecombe . irered habbe þ þere biside
A uair chapel of sein Kenelm . þat men seche þ wyde

St Kenelm 333-336

(Now it is beautifully covered, with a slab of limestone as it should be. May
every person who comes to this place be prepared to drink from it. Afterwards
the monks of Winchcombe erected beside it a beautiful chapel of St Kenelm,
which people come to visit from afar.)

Places like Winchcombe were the tangible evidence of God's power and
His love for the English people.

Although at first sight the legend of St Kenelm seems little more
than a fairytale-like story about a boy saint, the legend acquires a deeper
meaning when seen in the light of the legends about the English saints as a
group in the *South English Legendary*. Perhaps more strongly than in
any of the other legends, it expresses the longing for the old Anglo-Saxon
times when God's grace so openly rested upon England and its inhabi-
tants. Since the coming of the Norman kings who acted against the benefit
of the church, this grace is no more to be seen. Or, to quote the words of
Bishop Dunstan once more, it is *þe lond folk of Engelond . þat no gult
nabbe þ þerto* who suffer most.

REFERENCES

De Grijs, F.J.A. (1983). Heiligen, wat zijn dat eigenlijk? In: R.E.V. Stuip and C.
    Vellekoop (eds.). *Andere Structuren, Andere Heiligen.* Utrecht: HES. 13-32.
D'Evelyn, C., and A.J. Mill (eds.) (1956-59). *The South English Legendary.* 3 Vols.
    EETS, OS 235, 236, 244.
Görlach, M. (1973). *The Textual Tradition of the South English Legendary.* Leeds
    Texts and Monographs, New Series 6. Leeds.
Von Antropoff, R. (1965). *Die Entwicklung der Kenelm Legende.* Dissertation. Bonn.

HAVELOK THE DANE
A NON-COURTLY ROMANCE

HENK AERTSEN
(Free University, Amsterdam)

As Bennett points out (1986:121), the term 'romance' was first applied to classical and pseudo-classical narratives written in the vernacular language of France, such as the *Roman d'Enéas* and the *Roman de Thebes*, to distinguish them from their Latin originals. Thus a *roman* is a story in Latin on a classical subject that was *romanicé* or 'romanced', i.e. translated into French, and the word *roman* can therefore be rendered into Modern English simply as 'the French book' (cf. Everett, 1955:2).[1] At a later stage, the term 'romance', just like the OF *roman*, came to be used for "those tales of knights and their doings for which the French were first famous, without regard to the language in which they were written" (Everett, 1955:3).

A term related to 'romance' is *gest(e)*, which Bennett calls "a subspecimen of romance", indicating, he says, "that some historical truth is claimed for the narrative" (1986:121). The Middle English word *gest(e)*, usually rendered as 'narrative, story', is a borrowing from Old French and is ultimately derived from Latin *gesta* 'deeds, exploits; events'.

The terms 'romance' and 'geste' both occur in the romance under the discussion, *Havelok the Dane* [2] (henceforth *HD*). They are found al-

---

[1] A fuller derivation and explanation of the word *romance* is given by Baugh (1948: 173, note 1):

> The word *romance* comes from a Latin adverb *romanice*, meaning "in the Roman manner" (*loqui romanice*, to speak in the Roman manner, i.e. speak colloquial Latin). In time, with the change of Vulgar Latin into the various romance languages, it came to mean more particularly French, and then something written in French, especially something translated from Latin.

[2] All quotations from HD have been taken from the edition by Skeat as revised by Sisam (Skeat and Sisam, 1915). The poem has also been edited by Holthausen (1928), and by French and Hale (1964:71-176) and Schmidt and Jacobs (1980: i.37-121) for their anthologies, while annotated selections have appeared in most Middle English readers. A new authoritative, but rather expensive, edition by Smithers has recently been published (1987).

most side by side in the catalogue of royal entertainments which were part of the festivities following Havelok's coronation as king of Denmark:

> Hwan he was king, þer mouhte men se
> Þe moste ioie þat mouhte be: ...
> Romanz-reding on þe bok;
> Þer mouhte men here þe geste singe,
> Þe gleumen on þe tabour dinge.
>
>   (2320-21, 2327-29)

(When he was king, one could see there the greatest gaiety that could be: ... reading of romances in the book; there one could hear the stories being sung, and the minstrels beating the drum.)

We see that the poet speaks of 'reading of romances' and of 'singing of *gestes*', and this distinction is commented on by Schmidt and Jacobs in the following way (1980:i.184):

> The contrast seems to be one between works *read* out aloud (courtly 'romances' in French) and works *sung*, perhaps by the gleemen who strike the tabor ('gestes' in the language of the ordinary people). The *Havelok*-poet has called his own work a 'gest' (2989[3]) not a 'romanz' (which is probably what he would have called his French source, if he had one), but he can hardly have intended it to be 'sung'.

This interpretation of *gestes* does not seem to be consistent with their rendering of this word in the gloss at the foot of p.102, which reads "*gestes*, epics ('chansons de geste')", because what they say about the *Havelok* poet calling his own work a 'gest' is equally true of epics: epics can hardly have been intended to be sung either. French and Hale divide lines 2327-29 differently: whereas Schmidt and Jacobs link the singing of *gestes* to the minstrels or gleemen of the next line, French and Hale take the first two lines together and have no part for the drum-beating minstrels in the reading of romances or the singing of *gestes*, since their note

---

[3] The line-numbering in Schmidt and Jacobs' edition of *HD* differs from that in the edition from which we quote, the Skeat-Sisam edition.

to these lines reads (1964:152): "Note that some of the gestes here were sung; the readers and singers were the aristocrats among minstrels, and trick drummers were not their equals." In additon to the contrast between works to be read out and works to be sung, these notes by Schmidt and Jacobs and by French and Hale establish another contrast, although they do so less explicitly—it is a contrast between upper and lower-class audiences, i.e. the people of the court and the ordinary people. As Schmidt and Jacobs say in the note quoted above, "the *Havelok*-poet has called his own work a 'gest'", when he addresses his audience at the end of the poem in a kind of epilogue: *Nu haue ye herd þe gest al þoru / Of Hauelok and of Goldeborw* (ll.2984-85: 'Now you have heard the story of Havelok and Goldeboru completely, from beginning to end').

That the term 'gest' may also denote romances written for the lower classes, or for non-courtly audiences, is supported by *HD* and by the way in which it presents its subject-matter: Staines, for instance, says that the poet "addressed himself to a particular audience: the lower classes" (1976:612). The same idea had been expressed by others before Staines: Creek was one of the first to recognize the "homely and popular elements" in *HD*, but his conclusion that the poem "was intended not for the hall, but for the inn or street" (1915:210) is unfortunately based on the prologue and epilogue, which may be minstrel additions; yet he points out a great many homely details in other parts of the poem, as well as some homely figures of speech and proverbial expressions of "the folk", which suggest that "the English redactor was one with an intimate and sympathetic acquaintance with humble life" (1915: 207). *HD*, Creek says (1915:203), "seems to introduce us to the atmosphere of humble life of medieval England. There is no other English romance which does this to an equal extent, and there are scarcely any which do so at all." In other words, *HD* is at least in this respect unique, and this is also noted by Pearsall (1965:98):

> *Havelok* is unique among English romances in its systematic realisation of the story in terms of humble everyday life. (...) Havelok's qualities—his instinct for survival, opportunism, modesty, industry, lack of sentiment, practical good sense, love of children —are the virtues of common people. (...) *Havelok* has a claim, if any English romance has, to be regarded as the genuine expression of popular consciousness.

Hanning (1967:605) comes to a similar evaluation: "The meaning itself
... is no less impressive for being presented in a popular rather than a
courtly garb." Mehl's conclusion (1968:166) is that "There is no doubt
that the poem is addressed not to a courtly, but to a middle-class audience,
with the intention of appealing to a great variety of tastes."

Audience and subject-matter thus explain Schmidt and Jacobs'
characterization of *HD* as "a 'non-courtly' poem" (1980:i.8), but this
should come as no surprise, since Pearsall (1965:91) has shown that

> the social context of Middle English romance ... is overwhelm-
> ingly popular and non-courtly. True courtly romance had no real
> vogue in English, since the audience which could appreciate it, at
> the time when it was fashionable, was French-speaking. The only
> exceptions are the alliterative romances and the late adaptations of
> the genre by Chaucer. The audience of Middle English romances is
> primarily a lower or lower-middle class audience.

The poet also uses other terms with reference to the poem. In the prologue and epilogue he calls a *rym* (ll.21, 23, 2995, 2998), meaning "a
riming poem, song, or ballad; a verse narrative" according to the *MED*.
The Prologue also has the term *tale* (ll.3, 5 12), which is specifically used
for narratives delivered orally. A similar term is *spelle*, which occurs in
l.338: *Say we nou forth in ure spelle!* 'Let us now proceed with the telling
of our story!' The function of this line is to mark the transition between
the two introductory episodes of the poem, one being set in England and
dealing with the death of King Athelwold and the appointment of Earl
Godrich as the guardian of Athelwold's infant daughter Goldeboru, the
other describing similar events and a similar state of affairs in Denmark,
the death of King Birkabeyn and the appointment of Earl Godard as the
guardian of Birkabeyn's infant children Swanborough, Elfled and Havelok. Yet in spite of the specific function of this line in the poem, there is
no special meaning in the use of the word *spelle*, which is simply a term
that was "commonly used throughout the mediaeval period in England to
refer to speech and oral accounts in general" (Strohm, 1971:353).

Of the two terms *spelle* and *tale*, the latter was the more general,
according to Strohm, and was used even when the narrative could be de-
fined more narrowly as a *storie* (used in ll.1641 and 1734), *tretys*, or *lyf*
(i.e. saint's life, see below). *Spelle*, Strohm says, was "somewhat more

restricted in range, usually to oral narratives with limited scope and immediate impact" (1971:353). Both these qualifications may apply to the use of *spelle* in 1.338: the introductory episodes are of limited scope in that they set the scene and provide the background for the subsequent development of the plot, but they also have an immediate impact in that they make the audience side with the hero against his adversaries, the narrator acting as an intermediary in this respect (cf. Mehl, 1968:26, 167).

The title of Skeat's edition, *The Lay of Havelok the Dane*, suggests that Skeat considered the poem to be "an English equivalent to the Anglo-Norman *Lai d'Haveloc* (Bennett, 1986:154). It is true that the Anglo-Norman poem is called a *lai* in its opening lines, but this is only a trick, as Bennett explains, because the poet is "trying, like Chaucer with his *Franklin's Tale* much later, to pass off his poem as a Breton lay though in fact he based it on a known literary work, Gaimar's *Histoire des Engleis*" (1986:154-55). What is perhaps more important in this respect is that the Middle English poem is too different from the Anglo-Norman *Lai* to be considered an English equivalent to it. The Anglo-Norman poem is an upper-class or courtly romance, dealing with *noble fez* ('noble feats') and *l'aventure d'un riche rei / E de plusurs altres baruns* ('the adventure of a great king and of several other barons'), whereas in *HD* there is "the atmosphere of humble life of medieval England" (Creek, 1915:203). This difference is illustrated, for instance, by Grim, who is one of the barons in the Anglo-Norman *Lai*, but he is merely a fisherman in *HD*. The conclusion, therefore, can only be that the title of Skeat's edition is somewhat unfortunate.

In the manuscript the poem appears with the heading

Incipit Vita Hauelok quondam Rex Anglie et Denemarchie

(Here begins the Life of Havelok, formerly King of England and Denmark)

The term *vita* was the usual name for the genre known as the 'saint's life', and its application to the Havelok story gives rise to a number of interesting observations[4], of a speculative nature it is true, since it cannot be

---

[4] For some of these observations I am indebted to Schmidt and Jacobs (1980:i.7, 173). Their explanation of the implications of the term *vita* has been supplemented by me with the references to Creek, Staines, Mehl and *HD*, 1.12.

ascertained whether the Latin title is authentic (i.e. given by the poet) or whether it is the invention of the scribe who copied the manuscript. It is not altogether unusual for a romance to be entitled 'The Life of ...', as *Ipomadon B*, for instance, has this title, but the term *vita* has religious associations, which would suggest, if the title is the author's, that he was a cleric. This view would support Creek's conclusion (1915:211) that "the author belonged to the clergy", a conclusion he reached on the basis of "the emphasis [in the poem] on religious matters, the insistence on the moral aspects of the story, the love of proverbial wisdom" and especially because of "two scraps of Latin" in the poem, both of which are "of a religious character": *Benedicamus domino* (l.20: 'let us bless the Lord') and *"In manus tuas," loude he seyde* (l.228: '"Into your hands," he said loudly').

HD is followed by *King Horn* in MS Laud Misc. 108, where these two romances are preceded and followed by a number of saints' lives: the scribe may have felt that these two poems would not be out of place in a collection of saints' lives. Schmidt and Jacobs (1980:i.7) define the saint's life by its twofold purpose:

> to praise God by showing His marvellous works in the lives of chosen individuals, and to assure the audience that God's omnipresence often took the specific form of intervention in the lives of men, now loving, now vengeful.

These two aspects of a saint's life are both present in *HD*: "to praise God" is exactly what the poet (or scribe or minstrel) calls on his audience to do (l.20, quoted above), and Havelok may be regarded as "a divinely favoured individual in whose life God intervenes not on one but on several occasions" (Schmidt and Jacobs, 1980:i.7). This seems to link up well with the way in which Staines (1976:613) characterizes the poem:

> It is first and foremost an idealized biography cast in the form of a tale of action. The biography concentrates, not on the most exciting moments of Havelok's life, but rather on those episodes which delineate most clearly the poet's conception of the ideal king.

The ideal king is the good king, the king who "works for the welfare of his subjects, [who] is the protector of the poor, the orphaned, and the widowed, [who] is the provider of the lower classes, [who] must be a God-fearing individual, since the beginning of wisdom is fear of the Lord" (Staines, 1976:614[5]). Note how well this description of the good king fits the portrait of King Athelwold in *HD* (ll.27-105): the orphaned and the widowed are explicitly mentioned (ll.75, 79), and Athelwold *louede god with al his miht, And holi kirke, and soth, and riht* (ll.35-36: 'loved God with all his might, and the Holy Church, and truth and justice'). Athelwold, in other words, is the perfect Christian king, and at the end of the poem it is Havelok who is the right king power (cf. Weiss, 1969:249-50). The poem shows, as it were, how Havelok develops these innate qualities of the good and perfect king, and it is precisely these qualities that are emphasized in saints' lives.[6]

Mehl (1968:172) mentions another feature that *HD* shares with some of the saints' lives:

> the poem ... resembles the *vitae* of some saints in that it presents models of human behaviour and provides instruction as well as entertainment, in a more specific sense than can be said of the shorter romances. There is no 'escapism' in this poem.

"It ... provides instruction": this is in fact what the Prologue says the poem does: *And þe tale ye mowen y-lere* (l.12: 'And you can learn from the story'). However, it is also with respect to another important distinction between *vitae* or saints' lives and romances that *HD* seems more to resemble a *vita* than a romance: saints' lives describe historical persons (though their biographies may contain non-historical details), whereas romances do not, since they or most of them create a character and assign a given ideal to this fictitious character. Saints' lives and romances are therefore different in their respective starting-points: a saint's life starts from a historical person with an idealized quality, while a romance starts from an ideal and creates a fictitious character to represent this ideal. In the case of *HD*, the ideal is that of the good king (cf. the quote from

---

[5] Staines here paraphrases the description of the ideal king in John of Salisbury's *Policraticus*, a mid-twelfth-century political treatise, which may well have been the model for the political ideas underlying *HD*. Staines quotes and translates in footnotes the passages from the *Policraticus* which he paraphrases.

[6] Cf. Renée Hamelinck's study on "St Kenelm and the *South-English Legendary*" in this volume.

Staines above), and the historicity of the character of Havelok has been the subject of a long debate, which is summarized in the Skeat-Sisam edition of *HD* (pp.xxv-vi): the name *Havelok* may be a form of the Celtic name *Abloc* or *Abloec*, an adaptation of ON *Olaf-r*, OE *Anlaf*, in which case the name may refer to the "famous Viking, Olaf Sictricson, who was on the defeated side at Brunanburh in 937", but the section just referred in the Introduction to the Skeat-Sisam edition also mentions other potential candidates. The difference between a saint's life and a romance can be summed up in this way: the *vita* tells a story from the point of view of the person, the romance from that of the ideal, or, in the *vita* it is the person who speaks, in romance it is the ideal.

Schmidt and Jacobs (1980:i.1) give a rather simple defintion of the subject-matter of Middle English romances: "The medieval English romances are stories in verse which deal with the adventures of noble men and women and which end happily." They admit that this definition is vague, but it is good enough in view of the evidence. It is possible, they maintain, to establish certain prominent features as universal and defining features of the genre: 'fighting' or 'the marvellous' are common in romances, but by no means universal, as there is no fighting in *Floris and Blauncheflour* and *Athelston*, and 'the marvellous' is lacking in *Ipomadon*. Love is not a defining feature either: it "plays an important part in French but a smaller part in English romance"; nor is the 'courtly' tone such a feature: it is "found in the best single English romance, *Sir Gawain and the Green Knight*, but not in *Havelok*, which is arguably the second best" (1980:i.1).

Bennett (1986:122) has a similar general definition of the subject-matter of romances, and immediately adds that the romance under discussion, *HD*, does not conform to this description in two respects:

> Most romances, ..., narrate the adventures of some hero of chivalry. Yet the eponymous hero of *Havelok*, though of royal birth, can hardly be called such a hero. What such a tale has in common with the French romances from which so many English romances derive is the element of perilous adventure and feats of martial prowess. Love, which later ages were to associate with romance, plays a very minor part in *Havelok*.

There are, then, three respects in which *HD* stands out from the other Middle romances: its lack of a 'courtly' tone (cf. Creek's observation, quoted above, that there is in *HD* "the atmosphere of humble life in medieval England" [1915:203]), the absence of a noble hero, and the absence of love. On the other hand, it cannot be denied that Havelok *is* the hero and that his deeds are dealt with in the romance. That is why Mehl's description (1968:17) of the subject-matter of the Middle English romances—"Most of the Middle English romances are devoted to the glorification of some particular hero. This is not true of the French romances to the same extent."—is especially relevant to *HD*: Mehl refrains from speaking of a hero *of chivalry*, he simply says "hero", nor does he mention love as an important feature of romances.

There are various classifications of Middle English romances. The traditional classification is the one according to the cycles of stories on which the romances are based. It ultimately goes back to a passage in one of the poems of the late-twelfth-century French poet Jean Bodel, in which he speaks of *trois matières* ('three matters'), *de France et de Bretaigne et de Rome la grant* ('of France and of Britain and of Rome the great').[7] This division must have been unsatisfactory from the start, even if only applied to Bodel's own time and to the literature of his day, because it "very imperfectly sums up the riches and the variety of French romantic themes" and especially because "the 'matter of Rome' includes the whole of antiquity, the tales of Thebes and Troy, the wars of Alexander" (Ker, 1907:279). Wilson (1968:199) comments on the inadequacy of Bodel's division for the development of the genre during the following 200 years, when "a great number of new romance themes were introduced, mainly from the east... [which] are usually somewhat negligently grouped together as 'Miscellaneous Romances'. (...) In addition there grew up in England a class of romance peculiar to the country and based, though often very remotely, on the earlier history of England. In imitation of Bodel's classification these are usually grouped together under the title of the 'Matter of England'."In this classification according to narrative

---

[7] This passage has been quoted, among others, by Schofield (1906:145), by Baugh (1948:174), and also by Ker (1907:279, note 2):
Ne sont que trois matières à nul home attendant,
De France et de Bretaigne at de Rome la grant.
Jean Bodel, *Chanson de Saisnes*.

material *HD* obviously belongs to the 'Matter of England', even though the hero is a Dane, but one "whose fortunes are tied up with England and whose principal adventures take place on the island" (Baugh, 1948:175); we may add that the hero even rose to be king of England.

Mehl (1968:31-32) rejects the classification according to 'matters' on two grounds. Like Wilson, he feels that the term 'Miscellaneous Romances' does not do full justice to the romances that come under this heading only because they "have not necessarily anything in common beyond the fact that they cannot be fitted into any of the *matières*." His second reason for rejecting this kind of classification is of a more general nature: "in most cases there is no logical and unambiguous correspondence between material and form, between a certain story and a poem based on it." This seems to echo Pearsall's observation that whereas stories are the property of everyone, "a formal tradition is the property only of its practitioners, and it is through its formal and stylistic aspects ... that the history of romance can be most objectively analysed" (1965: 96). In this analysis Pearsall distinguishes between romances written in four-stress couplets and those in tail-rhyme, and this distinction, he says, "is a very real one, for it corresponds to a more fundamental division between 'epic romance' and 'lyric romance', the former more prosaic, realistic, historical and martial, the latter more emotive, more concerned with love, faith, constancy and the marvellous." In Pearsall's classification *HD* is grouped among the 'epic romances', even though "the marvellous" can be said to be represented in the poem in Havelok's so-called birth-marks (see below).

Mehl calls Pearsall's distinction between epic romance and lyric romance "somewhat questionable" (1968:269, note 21), and proposes a classification which is based on length and which distinguishes between 'shorter' and 'longer' works. He admits that this distinction may appear somewhat oversimplified but explains that "size is by no means an external feature. It conditions the treatment of the story, the dramatic movement and the narrative structure" (1968:36). He links the question of size to the practice of oral delivery. There appears to be a large group of poems of between five and twelve hundred lines, and if it is assumed "that a thousand lines can be comfortably read in about an hour (alliterative long-lines would take about twice as long), it follows that each of these poems probably would have been read in one sitting" (1968:36-37). Several poems are about twice that length and they may have been divided in half and read in two instalments. Mehl has found a passage in *The Seege or Batayle of Troy* to support his thesis. In this poem of about two thousand lines there is in one of the manuscripts a passage (ll.980-83) that indicates the half-way point and that includes a short blessing and, significantly, a call for drinks. This clearly suggests a break in the delivery. There are similar passages to be found in other poems, and on the whole the longer romances are far less close-knit than the shorter ones and are clearly divided into separate episodes, some of which could, if necessary, be omitted or read separately. In Mehl's view, the length of a poem has implications for its oral delivery, which in turn affects the structure of the poem.

In Mehl's classification *HD* comes under the heading of the 'longer romances': its length, 3001 lines, would call for delivery in three instalments (possibly two), but it is not easy to find more or less natural breaks after approximately a third and two thirds of the poem. On the other hand, the structure of the narrative suggests a division into episodes (indicated by changes in setting: England - Denmark - England - Denmark - England), but all these episodes are necessary for the plot, which would become unintelligble if they were omitted. Earlier, in the discussion of the word spelle (l.338), we have noted that this line separates the two introductory episodes, and the ten lines preceding l.338 round off the episode set in England. In this line 338 the poet directly addresses his audience, and with this line the story shifts from England to Denmark. At the next shift of setting there is a similar address to the audience: *As ye shulen nou forthward lere,/Yf that ye wilen þer-to here* (ll.731-32: 'As you shall learn as the story proceeds, if you will listen to it'). With this line the story moves back to England: the landing of Grim in Lincolnshire. When the poet next addresses his audience, a change of setting has already taken place: *Þat sholen ye forthward ful wel leren,/Yif þat ye wile þe storie heren* (ll.1640-41: 'That you shall learn indeed as the story proceeds, if you will listen to it'). The difficulty here is that one leaf has been cut out of the MS, containing 180 lines (1444-1625), and on this particular leaf the change of setting from England to Denmark must have been effected. At the fourth and final change of setting the audience is only indirectly addressed by the poet (there is no *ye* as in the other changes): *Of Grim bidde ich na more spelle. —/But whan Godrich herde telle, ...* (ll.2530-31: 'I ask leave to tell of Grim no more. — But when Godrich heard tell ...'). In the lines immediately preceding, Havelok, still in Denmark at the

time, has sworn to found a priory for the salvation of Grim's soul, in the
town where Grim was buried and which bears his name (ll.2528-29). The
poet then continues with the lines just quoted, and what Godrich had
heard was that Havelok, now King of Denmark, had arrived in England
to claim the throne. This transition from Denmark to England is therefore less clearly marked than the other transitions, but it is hinted at by
the poet's intervention.

There are, then, five distinct episodes in the poem, and all the transitions between them are marked by the poet addressing the audience.
However, none of these transitions occur after groups of approximately
one thousand lines, which Mehl considers the standard length for delivery
in one sitting, as we have seen. It may well be that the break between the
third and fourth episodes, occurring in the portion of the poem now lost,
was explicitly referred to by the poet, a break that would have come at
approximately the half-way point in the story. This would suggest a
reading of the poem in two sittings, and the second sitting would in that
case have involved the final two episodes, both of which are a kind of
climax in the narrative, the fourth episode dealing with Havelok winning
the crown of Denmark and with the execution of the false guardian
Godard, the fifth episode with Havelok winning the crown of England
and with the execution of the false guardian Godrich.

The oral delivery has affected not only the structure of the poem,
which is, as we have seen, made up of five distinct episodes, but it has also
affected the development of the plot, which we shall examine in some
detail, but it maay not be inappropriate to give a brief synopsis of the
poem first.

The story of *HD* is the story of two dispossessed young royal
orphans, a prince in Denmark, Havelok, and a princess in England,
Goldeboru. After their fathers, both of whom are depicted as good kings,
have died in the prime of their lives, Havelok and Goldeboru are each left
in the hands of a supposedly good guardian, who proves treacherous,
however, in wishing to usurp the throne. In the end Havelok vanquishes
both the Danish and the English usurper and recovers the two kingdoms
for himself and Goldeboru, who had become his wife.

The plot of *HD* shows, according to Hanning (1967:588) three
common elements of romance plots: (1) the hero's movement from loss
to recovery—this is the most common element of the romance plot, and it

also covers the device of the discovery of 'real identity'; (2) the hero's development from immaturity or faultiness to maturity and perfection; and (3) a love relationship which unites the hero (in his deprived and/or developing state) and a heroine who has also been the victim of deprivation or other injustice. These three plot elements which are clearly interrelated have been unified by the poet into a narrative with an artistic structure, as we shall see.

On the level of the plot the oral delivery of the poem manifests itself in the recurrence of a number of symbols and acts which are central to the theme of the poem and to the development of the plot. This recurrence is frequently realized by means of verbal repetitions, which the poet employs for a twofold purpose: through these repetitions he not only provides the audience with easy points of reference, enabling them to link a given passage to an earlier passage, but through these repetitions he can also communicate to his audience the importance of what they have just heard or are about to hear. In other words, the verbal repetitions, and recurrences in general for that matter, have both a unifying function (with regard to structure) and an emphatic function (with regard to plot and narrative).

This twofold purpose is illustrated by the first two episodes of *HD*, which deal with similar events in England and Denmark (for an outline of these episodes, see the discussion of the word *spelle* above), and which therefore constitute the first instance of repetition on a large scale. The first episode narrates how a young and helpless heiress is stripped of her rights (and thereby of her future) by a strong and wicked adult[8], and the second episode narrates the same process with regard to a young and helpless heir. Why did the poet opt for this double statement of misery and misfortune? We have already given a possible answer when we said that the opening episodes make the audience side with the hero against his adversaries, and in this way the poet assures himself of the continued attention of his audience, since they have now become involved in the story. But there is more to these first two episodes. The double statement of misfortune serves to emphasize the contrast between the helplessness of youth and the power of adulthood, and Hanning (1967:590) sees in this

---

[8] Note that at the end of the first episode we have yet to meet the hero of the poem. This may seem strange in the light of the poet's announcement in the Prologue that *Þe tale of Hauelok is i-maked* (l.5: "the story is about Havelok'), yet we shall demonstrate that Havelok figures prominently, though indirectly of course, in this episode.

contrast a direct reference to two of "the central movements of the Havelok story", the movement from loss to recovery and the complementary
movement from youth to maturity (mentioned above as two common elements of romance plots): "By linking youth and loss twice in quick succession ..., *Havelok the Dane* unmistakably announces the thematic inter-
ests which control its narrative progress." The movement from loss to
recovery is marked off by two almost identical lines, the first symbol-
izing Havelok's loss, the second his recovery. The first of these lines occurs when the wicked Earl Godard has slaughtered Havelok's two sisters
and is about to do the same to Havelok, who, kneeling before Godard, ask
for mercy, saying

> Manrede, louerd, biddi you!
>   (484)
>
> (Feudal homage, lord, I offer you!)

With these words Havelok surrenders his sovereignty and becomes a vas-
sal to the earl, who he now recognizes as his lord. By offering homage to
Godard, Havelok symbolically (and therefore implicitly) denies his social
identity as heir to the Danish throne, which in turn leads to his explicit
loss of personal identity in leaving Denmark to grow up as a fisherman's
son in England (cf. Hanning, 1967:592). Line 484 thus symbolizes the
low point of the story, and it is to be related to the second occurrence of
this particular line in the poem, slightly modified but with essentially the
same meaning: *Manred, louerd, bede y þe* (1.2172: 'Feudal homage, lord,
I offer you'). Here the person addressed is Havelok, and the words are
spoken by Ubbe, a great Danish earl who had been a close friend of
Havelok's father, King Birkabeyn. Having seen Havelok's birth-marks
(on which we comment below), this Ubbe recognizes him as "*Birka-
beynes sone*" (1.2150: 'Birkabeyn's son') and realizes that he is the rightful heir to the Danish throne ("*he is hise eyr*", 1.2157: 'he is his [i.e. Birkabeyn's] heir'); then Ubbe and his men fall on their knees and offer
homage to Havelok with the words of line 2172, which is therefore symbolic of the moment of recovery, and at this point the main action of *HD*
is completed. The moment of recovery does not have to coincide with
Havelok's coronation as King of Denmark, because he was not yet king
when he offered homage to Godard. Note that the order of the final steps

towards the moment of recovery is the exact opposite of that of the consequences of the loss:

    A. the loss
        1. Havelok's feudal homage to Godard, i.e. his giving up his sovereignty;
        2. his loss of social identity;
        3. his loss of personal identity.
    B. the recovery
        1. Havelok's recovery of personal identity (l.2150);
        2. his recovery of social identity (l.2157);
        3. Ubbe's feudal homage to Havelok (l.2172), restoring Havelok's sovereignty.

Note also that about half-way between lines 484 and 2172 there is a first indication that Havelok is well on the way to recover what he had lost. It occurs after Havelok has fled with his wife Goldeboru from Lincoln to Grimsby and is received by Grim's children who surrender themselves to him: *Þou maght us boþe selle and yeue; / Þou maght us boþe yeue and selle, / With-þat þou wilt here dwelle* (ll.1218-20: 'You might both sell and give us [i.e. into slavery]; you might both give and sell us, on condition that you stay here'). They also turn over all their property to him: *Bi-leue her, louerd, and al be þin!* (l.1228: 'Stay here, lord, and everything will be yours!'), and next they accept him as their lord: *Þou shalt ben louerd, þou shalt ben syre,/ And we sholen seruen þe and hire.* (ll. 1229-30: 'You shall be lord, you shall be sir, and we shall serve you and her [i.e. Goldeboru]'.) However, Havelok's installation as head of the Grim household is more than a first sign of the process of recovery being well under way: it also points forward to Havelok's eventual coronation as King of Denmark, since the Grim household, a Danish family in exile in England, symbolically stands for the Danish nation, and their acceptance of Havelok as *paterfamilias* thus has symbolic significance. This scene also points backwards, as it echoes the words spoken by Grim after he had witnessed the first manifestations of Havelok's 'birth-marks' and prophesied

> þis ure eir
> Þat shal ben louerd of Denemark,

He shal ben king, strong and stark;
He shal hauen in his hand
Al Denemark and Engeland.
(606-10)

(This is our heir who shall be lord of Denmark, he shall be king, strong and
stout; he shall have in his power all of Denmark and England.)

And Grim then does homage to Havelok:

Louerd, haue merci
Of me, and Leue, þat is me bi!
Louerd, we aren boþe þine,
Þine cherles, þine hine.
(617-20)

(Lord have mercy on me and on Leue, who is standing beside me! Lord, we
are both yours, your thralls and your servants.)

Thus, the homage which Grim offers the child Havelok is as it were reaf-
firmed by Grim's children when they do homage to the grown-up
Havelok, and it is this difference in Havelok's age that makes this reaffir-
mation more effective and symbolically significant.

The repetition of 1.484 in 1.2172 and the reverse patterning of the
elements involved in the processes of loss and recovery betray the skill of
a great story-teller, one who knew how to relate plot to structure. This is
equally apparent from the way in which he handles the second thematic
movement, the hero's development from an immature youth to a mature
adult. Such a process of growth must be gradual, and therefore it cannot
have the clear beginning and ending of the first thematic movement.
Consequently it must consist of a series of recurring incidents, each of
them symbolzing a particular phase in this process of growth to adulthood. Hanning (1967:594) has identified these recurring incidents with
symbolic meaning, which are of three kinds: (1) feasts; (2) feats of
strength; and (3) revelations of Havelok's birth-marks. They are interrelated in the sense that a feast often follows a feat of strength and/or a
revelation of birth-marks, and this interrelation is further evidence of the
poet's skill.

In medieval romance feasts and, more generally, dinners, often have a particular symbolic function.[9] In *HD* there are no less than six occasions on which food is consumed, and although the first two of them are hardly feasts, since they lack the ceremonial and social aspects inherent in a feast, they all occur at crucial moments in the story and signal important stages in the hero's development to adulthood. In this series of meals and feasts there is a kind of progression that runs parallel to Havelok's growth to adulthood: each meal is more important than the previous one, and this is reflected in the food served at each meal—just as the meals become more and more important, the food becomes richer and richer. The sixth and final meal in the series, Havelok's coronation feast in England, is described by the poet in only three lines (ll.2948-50), which seems to indicate that the poet regarded this sixth feast as relatively unimportant (cf. his elaborate treatment of Havelok's coronation feast in Denmark, ll. 2320-45), no doubt because it falls outside the poem's thematic movement, the hero's development to adulthood and maturity having been completed with the coronation feast in Denmark. Table I, which is based on Hanning (1967:594-98), summarizes this series of meals and feasts and specifies the symbolic significance of each meal or feast to the hero's development to adulthood.

The second series of recurring incidents that is symbolic of Havelok's growth to adulthood is that of his feats of strength, which he performs on three occasions. Havelok's strength is repeatedly mentioned (e.g. l.829: *For he was strong*; ll.988-90: *He was boþe stark and strong; / In Engelond was non his per / Of strengþe* 'He was both stout and strong;

---

[9] In *Sir Gawain and the Green Knight*, for instance, each of the two dramatic movements making up the plot, the Beheading Game and the Exchange of Gifts, has a dinner or a series of dinners as the setting for its initial or central action. In the case of the Beheading Game it is the Christmas dinner at Arthur's court, the first course of which had hardly been served when the Green Knight came riding into the hall at Camelot (ll.135-36). The Green Knight's challenge for *a Crystemas gomen* (l.283: 'a Christmas game') creates a dramatic tension which is only partially relieved by his subsequent beheading, and therefore interferes with the joyous atmosphere of the Christmas dinner. (This is not the place to go into the symbolic significance of the relation between the dinner and the challenge and beheading.) Similarly, the Exchange of Gifts, agreed upon by Gawain and his host Bertilak for the duration of Gawain's stay at Hautdesert, takes place immediately before dinner on three consecutive nights (ll.1372-1401, 1623-57, 1932-56). These dinners serve to emphasize the fellowship between host and guest, just as the Exchange of Gifts is a gesture of fellowship (see Burrow, 1965:95, and Aertsen, 1987:98-100).

FEAST	LINES	SETTING	OCCASION	SYMBOLIC SIGNIFICANCE
1	634-56	Grim's cottage (in Denmark)	after the planned murder of H. by Grim is prevented by the first revelation of the two signs of his royal descent; Grim accepts H. as his lord	the first concrete sign that H. has stepped back from the brink of death; the feast/meal acts to restore his famished body
2	921-30	the kitchen of the Earl's Cook in Lincoln	after H. is hired by the Cook to carry his baskets of fish	H.'s first independent and competitive steps in the world; again the feast/meal acts to restore his famished body
3	1237-46	the house of Grim's children at Grimsby	after H. is accepted by Grim's children as their lord	central function in the story: points back to Grim's acceptance of H. (see 1) and forward to H.'s coronation as King of Denmark (see 5)
4	1714-29	the castle of Ubbe, a Danish earl and close friend of H.'s father	H., pretending to be a merchant, is granted permission by Ubbe to make a living in his district, gives the earl a gold ring (cf. note 9); Ubbe suspects that H. is more than he claims to be and invites H. and his company to a dinner	H. is back in Denmark and is on the threshold of the victory toward which he had been maturing since the first night and meal in Grim's cottage
5	2340-45	not identified in the poem—probably Ubbe's castle	H.'s coronation banquet, preceded by games and tournaments, songs and minstrelsy	this banquet highlights the series of feasts: H., now King of Denmark, has regained all that he had lost earlier
6	2948-50	London	H.'s coronation feast in England	relatively unimportant: falls outside the poem's thematic movement (see text)

Table I

Meals and Feasts in *HD*

[H. = Havelok]

in England no one was his equal in strength'), and Havelok has thus fulfilled what Grim had prophesied about him after the revelation of his birth-marks in Grim's hut: *he shal ben king, strong and stark* (1.608: 'he shall be king, stout and strong'). Table II lists these feats of strength and specifies their symbolic significance.The many references to Havelok's strength are what one might expect of a romance hero, but in his growth to adulthood it is not sufficient that he should be strong—in the contests and fights in which he engages he should come out the winner: that is what one expects of a future king and that is why 1.608 is a key line in the poem. Note that, as in the series of feasts, there is a kind of progression in Havelok's feats of strength: when he first fights his way to the job of basket carrier for the Earl's Cook, he overcomes "nine or ten" rivals (1.871), the next day he beats as many as sixteen of them (1.890) and the number of thieves who attack Bernard's house is given as 61 in 1.1918. As the opposition increase, Havelok's feats become more and more impressive. Note also that in the descriptions of the victorious Havelok the poet emphasizes not only his physical strength but also his social qualities—gentleness, generosity and justice: ll.930-44 describe his physical strength, ll.945-58 his social qualities (cf. 1.945: *Of alle men was he mest meke* 'Of all men he was gentlest'). The poet links this description of Havelok's social qualities to the description of King Athelwold in the first introductory episode: ll.955-56 (*Him loueden alle, stille and bolde, / Knihtes, children, yunge and olde* 'Everybody, shy and bold, loved him, knights, children, young and old') echo 1.30 (*Him louede yong, him louede olde* 'Young and old loved him'), as if to indicate that Havelok has by now developed the qualities of a good and just king. When the poet speaks of Havelok's fame after the games at Lincoln, he combines these two aspects into a single line: *Hu he was strong and ek ful meke* (1.1066: 'how strong he was , and also how very gentle'). Finally it worth noting that there is a subtle touch of irony in the passage dealing with Godrich's decision to have Goldeboru marry Havelok: it was not only to fulfil his promise to the dying Athelwold that Goldeboru was to marry "the best, the fairest, and also the strongest man alive" (ll.198-200) but also to ensure himself and his son after him of the English throne (ll.1073-76), yet Goldeboru's marriage to Havelok is *not* disgraceful, and it does *not* ensure Godrich of the throne, it has precisely the opposite effect, as it in fact leads to his downfall.

The third series of recurring incidents that, together with the feasts and the feats of strength, symbolize Havelok's growth to adulthood is that

FEAT	LINES	SETTING	OCCASION	SYMBOLIC SIGNIFICANCE
1a 1b	871-78 889-92	Lincoln	pushing aside his competitors ("nine or ten" the first day, "sixteen" the next) for a job as carrier of baskets of fish for the Earl's Cook	this feat wins H. food in a time of famine (his second feast) and a steady job (his first independent steps in the world); the poet also stresses his social qualities (ll.945-58; see text)
2	979-1058	the games at Lincoln	ordered by the Cook to compete, H. wins the contest by "putting the stone" further than anyone else	this feat wins H. great fame (ll.1059-66); when Godrich hears of it, he makes Goldeboru marry H. (see text for details and for the irony involved)
3	1766-1919	at the house of Bernard, the magistrate in the town where Ubbe lives	H. is sent to Bernard by Ubbe to make sure that he and his wife will not be harmed, but Bernard's house is attacked by a gang of sixty thieves; H. kills them all with the help of the sons of Grim	Bernard, telling Ubbe of H.'s feat, emphasizes that H. saved his life and goods (ll.1974f, 2002-5); taking H. back to his own castle, Ubbe discovers H.'s real identity during the night, after witnessing H.'s birth-marks

Table II: Havelok's Feats of Strength

	LINES	SETTING	OCCASION	SYMBOLIC SIGNIFICANCE
1	588-605	Grim's cottage in Denmark	Grim is about to carry out Godard's order to kill H.	it saves his life, discloses H.'s real identity; Grim prophesies that H. shall be king of Denmark and England
2	1251-57	bedroom in the house of Grim's children	after the feast (no.3) H. and Goldeboru go to bed	it reveals his identity to his wife, who has the marks interpreted by an angel who repeats Grim's prophecy
3	2090-2147	Ubbe's castle	during the night following feat no.3	it reveals his identity to Ubbe, who does homage to him and dubs him a knight; H. is then made King of Denmark

Table III: Manifestations of Havelok's Birth-Marks

of the revelation of his *kyne-mark* (1.604: 'sign of his royal rank', i.e. the mark on his right shoulder) and the flame from his mouth, which are commonly referred to as Havelok's 'birth-marks'. There are three occasions on which these birth-marks are revealed so as to disclose the true identity of the hero, and they are listed in Table III, together with their symbolic significance. Note that on two of the three occasions the revelation of Havelok's birth-marks is followed by the prophecy that he shall be king of Denmark and England—first it is Grim who says so (ll.608-10), and then it is the angel interpreting the birth-marks for Goldeboru (ll.1265-74; in the angel's prophecy there is yet another instance of verbal repetition in the poem, as 1.1271 repeats 1.608 verbatim). On the third occasion that Havelok's identity is disclosed Ubbe does homage to Havelok (which marks the moment of recovery) and then promises that Havelok shall be king of Denmark (1.2178)—this time it is not a prophecy because Ubbe at once takes the necessary steps to fulfil his promise.

The intricate plot with its two thematic movements and with the interrelationships between the series of recurring incidents making up the second movement, and the verbal repetitions throughout the poem show that the poet was a great story-teller; if his verse had been of the same high quality, *HD* would have been one of the finest Middle English poems.

REFERENCES

Aertsen, H. (1987). *Play in Middle English. A Contibution to Word Field Theory.* Amsterdam: Free University Press.
Baugh, A.C. (1948). *A Liteary History of England.* London: Routledge and Kegan Paul.
Bennett, J.A.W. (1986). *Middle English Literature.* Ed. D. Gray. The Oxford History of English Literature, Vol.I, Part 2. Oxford: O.U.P.
Burrow, J.A. (1965). *A Reading of* Sir Gawain and the Green Knight. London: Routledge and Kegan Paul.
Creek, H.L. (1915). The Author of *Havelok the Dane. Englische Studien* 48. 193-212.
Everett, D. (1955). A Characterisation of the English Mediaeval Romances. In: *Essays on Middle English Literature.* Ed. P. Kean. Oxford: O.U.P. 1-22.
French, W.H. and C.B. Hale (eds.) (1964). *Middle English Metrical Romances.* 2 Vols. New York: Russell and Russell. (1st publ., 1930.)

Hanning, R.W. (1967). *Havelok the Dane*: Structure, Symbols, Meaning. *Studies in Philology* 64. 586-605.

Holthausen, F. (ed.) (1928). *Havelok*. 3rd ed. Alt- und Mittelenglische Texte I. Heidelberg: Carl Winter. (1st ed., 1901.)

Ker, W.P. (1907). Metrical Romances, 1200-1500. I. In: *The Cambridge History of English Literature*. Ed. A.W. Ward and A.R. Waller. Vol. I. Cambridge: C.U.P. 277-300.

Mehl, D. (1968). *The Middle English Romances of the Tirteenth and Fourteenth Centuries*. London: Routledge and Kegan Paul.

Pearsall, D. (1965). The Development of Middle English Romance. *Mediaeval Studies* 27. 91-116.

Schmidt, A.V.C. and N. Jacobs (eds.) (1980). *Medieval English Romances*. 2 Vols. London: Hodder and Stoughton.

Schofield, W.H. (1906). *English Literature from the Norman Conquest to Chaucer*. London: Macmillan.

Skeat, W.W. and K. Sisam (eds.) (1915). *The Lay of Havelok the Dane*. 2nd rev. ed. Oxford: O.U.P. (1st ed., 1902.)

Smithers, G.V. (ed.) (1987). *Havelok*. Oxford: O.U.P.

Staines, D. (1976). Havelok the Dane: A Thirteenth-Century Handbook for Princes. *Speculum* 51. 602-23.

Strohm, P. (1971). *Storie, Spelle, Geste, Romaunce, Tragedie*: Generic Distinctions in the Middle English Troy Narratives. *Speculum* 46. 348-59.

Weiss, J. (1969). Structure and Characterisation in *Havelok the Dane*. *Speculum* 44. 247-57.

Wilson, R.M. (1968). *Early Middle English Literature*. 3rd ed. London: Methuen. (1st ed., 1939.)

FLORIS AND BLAUNCHEFLOUR
TO INDULGE THE FANCY AND TO HEAR OF LOVE

N.H.G.E. VELDHOEN
(University of Leiden)

J.W.H. Atkins (1907:301) prefaces his discussion of the Middle English metrical romances by pointing out that

> the *raison d' être* of the romances is of a secular kind. It was felt to be good to indulge the fancy and to hear of love, and so legendary and historical narratives and cheerful love-stories were, from time to time, related with no other motive than the telling of a good tale.

Although *Floris and Blauncheflour* (henceforth *Fl & Bl*) is perhaps not, in the strictest sense, a romance—it is not a story of knight-errantry—yet the story of the two young lovers is told in the conventional narrative technique of the genre of the romance of chivalry. And Atkins' well-considered words will appear to apply particularly to this tale.

The point about the genre of *Fl & Bl* needs to be made because for the modern reader, conditioned by the modern novel or short story with their realistic verisimilitude, the kind of narrative to which *Fl & Bl* belongs is not immediately accessible. The story may be compelling enough, but the full impact of the medieval English rendering of this story will not be grasped unless one is ready and willing to accept a high degree of formality in it, which constitutes its own peculiar logic and significance.

Romances are stories of public life: they portray the age's ideals of life, of men and women, of what makes life significant. Underlying the romances is the assumption that rituals, when performed in the proper manner, add significance to life, or rather bring out the significance that life had in the theological culture of those days. And this is not only true for religious or courtly rituals, nor only for public or special rituals, but as much for what we would consider private or common rituals. For them such distinctions are immaterial. Swooning in public or in private, eating, asking the way, playing chess, as rituals properly performed, add as much significance to the life portrayed as the selection of a queen or the Christian marriage-ceremony.

This medieval sense of ceremony, i.e. formality as a way of celebrating significance in life, is reflected in the formality of construction of these tales. In *Fl & Bl* the formality is immediately apparent in the ritualistic repetitions: there are several innkeepers, several guides, several obstacles to be overcome, several disguises, even the game of chess is to be played three times. Also words and lines are repeated in the same ritualistic way: from the characteristic *vnne þes* ('reluctantly', ll.63 and 153) to describe Floris' father, to Floris' equally characteristic reaction when he is offered food:

> Mi þouʒt is, on alle wise,
> Mochel on mi marchaundise,
> And ʒit þat is mi meste wo
> ʒif ich hit finde and schal forgo.
> (ll.503-06)

(My thinking is in every way much engaged upon my merchandise, and yet that is my greatest anxiety, if I should find it and be obliged to do without it.)

These lines are repeated almost verbatim in ll.589-94.[1]

But the formality, the sense of ceremony in this kind of narrative, also accounts for such details as seem necessary for the plot: the second ring, the details of food eaten (ll.569-76), the blankets only pulled down a little to ascertain the sexes of the lovers in bed (ll.1059-62), the Emir marrying Clarice in the end.

Where we finally need this notion of formality most, where we need to see and accept the absolute dominance of the medieval sense of ceremony, is in our reading of those details which, in a modern narrative, should be noted as inconsistent in the story: the Oriental and pagan Emir is given West European chivalric paraphernalia. This unnatural despot has his city guarded by knights; he allows himself to be guided by a council of barons, placing chivalric honour over despotic judgment; he dubs Floris a knight and even administers a Christian marriage.

---

[1] All quotations from *Fl & Bl* have been taken from the edition by Taylor (1927).

In other words, the spirit or mood in which we are required to enjoy and interpret such stories is that with which we also approach fairy tales and folktales. They have the "feel" of the dream world: in a dream one can fly, and that causes no surprise, yet the feeling is memorable. And they have the logic of ritual games: the logic that makes us avoid the black lines with our feet when stepping across a zebra crossing. It is the symbolic logic of life experienced as basic desires and fears, and the ritual patterns ensuing from that.

In such narratives we are not shocked by what in modern stories should be considered as cruelty. In *Sir Gawain and the Green Knight* the beheading game does not unduly worry us. Neither need we be surprised in *Fl & Bl* to find Floris' father so murderously inclined. When on two occasions he proposes to have Blauncheflour killed (ll.45-51 and 141), he is speaking as the King who must insist on a fitting marriage-partner for his successor. And apart from this ritual aspect of his conduct, he is at the same time acting out the part of the father as rival or restrainer of his son's maturing sensuality. It is interesting to notice that by the side of the father's cruel effectiveness it is Floris' mother, or rather the King's wife, whose role it is to introduce more civilized alternatives. She proposes to send Floris away for some time *þat he lese not his honour / For þe mayden Blauncheflour* ('in order that he will not lose his honour because of the young girl Blauncheflour', ll.57-58) and later proposes the ruse of selling the girl away and pretending that she is dead (ll.144-52). It is characteristic that in both cases the King submits *vnne þes* ('reluctantly', ll.63 and 153), just as in similar instances later on he submits reluctantly to his wife and son: *Sen it may noon other be* ('since it may not be otherwise', l.322) and *Seth it is soo,/ Se þ þou wylt noon other doo* ('since that is how it is, since you will not do otherwise', ll.351-52). So love as a civilizing influence on the harsh man's world of public interest is shown to gain a hard-won victory. Similarly in the end the emir appears easily moved by the young lovers and ready to have a civilized trial rather than summary justice (ll.1109-30).

The Queen's loving influence does not stop at civilizing her husband's attitude and thereby granting full development to their son. She is also shown literally to give life to her son when she prevents his suicide at Blauncheflour's alleged grave. And symbolically she also gives life to Blauncheflour by opening the grave and showing that the girl is still alive (ll.308-40). This ultimate act of love wins the field for the lovers.

Fl & Bl is undeniably a story of love, although John Stevens rightly remarks (1973:44) that in contrast to other romances love here is not "all dark passion" or "merely businesslike":

> Amongst the English romances which seem to concede most to amorous ideals is *Fl & Bl*. But the concessions are more to sentiment than to *amour*. (...) Floris and Blancheflur are counters in a game of sentiments.

Every reader knows the sentiments of Ideal Love. We all know what to expect and wish for. And that is dramatized in the romances. But first and foremost we are aware of the obstacles, of our fears and misgivings. And those are dramatized primarily in the romances, and give them their shape of a series of conflicts. Our hopes are reflected in the fact that the hero invariably wins through. But the interest lies in the fears portrayed in action. These are the real points of recognition and of identification. Floris' parents and the gatekeeper and the Emir are in a way more real to our experience than Floris himself can ever be.

The love-interest in the Middle English romances operates on various levels. One level is that of strongly felt human relationships. On another, love is an ennobling and civilizing force. On again another love is the inspiration to transcend one's present self by means of action on behalf of a lady. This is love as part of the process of growing up, of growing away from self-centredness and mere self-assertion towards a civilized social identity. *Fl & Bl* shows that achieved love leads to social integrity: Floris and Blauncheflour's first free acts are acts of loyalty to the other characters involved. Floris loyally protects his 'man', the gatekeeper, from the Emir's wrath (ll.1245-50)—appropriately before he himself becomes the Emir's 'man', thus avoiding a clash of loyalties—and Blauncheflour intercedes for her trusted friend Clarice, achieving final harmony in the form of a marriage between Clarice and the Emir (ll.1277-79).

In the romance-manner of story-telling all the action and all the other characters are to be seen as reflecting the development of the protagonist. Therefore it is in Floris that we see the "education" that leads to the perfect love achieved in the end. And typically, his love-education follows the pattern of what from classical antiquity had been recognized as man's fundamental desires: his *libido*. That *libido* had been split into three kinds or levels: the *libido sciendi* ('the desire to know'), the *libido dominandi* ('the desire to dominate'), and the *libido sentiendi* ('the desire to feel, to be emotionally involved'). We can recognise the *libido sciendi* in the emphasis on Floris' going to school and on his being so dependent on instructions from others to achieve his ends. Floris receives directions and is taught the tricks—here in the form of plots and ruses—how to cope with "life". The *libido dominandi* is brought out in his many struggles against repression, in which he successively overcomes his parents, the gatekeeper, and finally, in a sense, the Emir. And in a love-story such as *Fl & Bl* the *libido sentiendi* is dominantly present. Floris' quest for his chosen love-partner is a quest for integrity, for a place and an identity in the grown-up world. The *libido sentiendi* is brought out by Floris' trying to achieve a pattern of relatedness and mutual loyalties. The enforcing of the truth at Blauncheflour's tomb and the struggle over who shall have the protective ring are the dramatic highlights of this narrative vein.

Having established the basic pattern of the ideal experience, there now remains to be seen of what nature the characters are in this formal world, and what the nature is of the "adventures" to which they are submitted.

We see Floris growing from child to independent man and master of men. That this is a difficult and painful process is illustrated by the fact that on seven different occasions on the way Floris does the unmanly thing: he weeps, either for frustration or fear or joy (ll.15-17; 83; 270; 847; 932; 947; 1134). This pattern of growth might have made for dramatic variety and tragic depth, as it had done in the epic narratives that preceded romances in time. But neither is to be found. The hero is a stereotype 'flat' protagonist, for the interest lies in the action, not in the character of the hero. He is an embodiment of virtue or of growth towards virtue. His story cannot be tragic, because if he dies, the virtue he embodies perishes with him, whereas romance sets out to show the virtue literally for what it is worth. This does not mean that there is nothing explorative to romances. Yet the character of the hero is 'flat'. The tensions and conflicting motives underlying the ideals are brought out by the action, not by dramatic conflicts within the character. The action is the full drama of the portrayed ideal, and the various characters , including the hero, personify various facets of the complex experience of trying to attain that ideal. The hero enacts the striving towards the pure ideal, while the other characters are representatives of the checks imposed by 'reality' and by the co-existence of other fundamental passions. Because the protagonist is the example or 'type' aimed at, all characters other than the protagonist are only important in relation to the protagonist, not in relation to each other. They 'are' the action.

The character of Floris is a *persona*, a 'mask'. We do not see an individual character experiencing 'reality' in his own particular way. The fact that he has a name does not make him an individual. In Floris we see an ignorant and dependent young boy winning through to a socially acceptable position. And we see him also developing. While he has to be shown his way most of the time, we see him taking the initiative twice, at crucial points: after the ruse of Blauncheflour's faked tomb has been exploded, Floris himself decides that he shall set out to find the girl, and he states his own terms of how he proposes to travel and what he will take with him; and ultimately it is the spontaneous act of endlessly exchanging the protective ring that overcomes the Emir. And yet Floris remains more or less the ignorant helpless child he was from the start.

This apparent inconsistency of a character showing development and yet remaining largely what he was from the beginning is typical of all romance heroes. They "go through the motions", but only to show that, and how, the ideal they represent overcomes all tests. The tests are not really moments of doubt, but elements that serve to define the nature of the ideal portrayed in action.

The term 'flat' suits the other characters in this narrative better. They are static: they cannot be 'educated'. They are representations of the perennial fears attendant upon Floris' ideal social personality. Floris' father and the gatekeeper and the Emir introduce into the action all these uncivilized desires that are incompatible with what Floris stands for. They constitute the primitive, uncontrolled and animal parts of the human being against which the protagonist is tested. They are the antagonists proper to Floris: they define him.

On his way to find himself, the ideal lover Floris overcomes three antagonists to that ideal: his father, the gatekeeper, and the Emir. His father represses his striving for integrity in the form of union with his appropriate partner Blauncheflour on the grounds of social conventions. These conventions of the impropriety of marriage between people of unequal birth—here pushed to the absolute of murder to prevent that— are represented as unfitting for the type of love that *Fl & Bl* idealizes.

The gatekeeper represses Floris' progress towards the achievement of his love on the grounds of a peculiar symbolic rivalry, which I will discuss later on. He has the peacock appearance of the typical rival lover: *þe porter is proud wiþalle;/ Euerich dai he goþ in palle* ('besides, the gatekeeper is proud: he is dressed in a rich robe every day', ll.679-80). Moreover, he is portrayed as jealous:

> Wel sone he wil come to þe
> And aske what mister man þou be
> And ber vpon þe felonie,
> And saie þou art comen þe tour aspie.
> (ll.753-56)

(Very soon he will come up to you and ask what business you have there, and accuse you of malicious intentions, saying you have come to spy on the tower.)

To this Floris is advised to reply with the meekness befitting the true lover: *þou shalt answeren him swetelich / And speke to him wel mildelich* ('you must answer him graciously and speak to him meekly', ll.757-58).

The medieval ideal lover will especially have to overcome the Emir, because the uncivilized type of love represented by him does certainly not fit the European ideal of the day. The Emir is not chivalrous to his ladies, whom he buys in the first place. He would be well described by the modern term 'male chauvinist pig': his 'love' is all lust and, one assumes, businesslike procreation, without any sense of relationship towards his partner. And that would be unacceptable to the mainly female audiences of Eleanor of Aquitaine's generation.

Quite appropriately Floris' antagonists are all male, because the checks to the ideal he portrays are aspects of the male psyche. The female characters in *Fl & Bl*, for their part, are manifestations of various aspects of the nature of Woman, at least of the idea of Woman in a man's mind. That idea appears to be mainly a set of complements to his own nature. Such complements can, in general, as easily enhance the beneficial as the malevolent aspects of his world. But in the love-romance *Fl & Bl* the female characters typically represent the positive influence on the male world. Floris' women add a whole range of experience of feminine virtue to the ideal action.

Blauncheflour is, throughout, a young lover's projection of an ideal love. She is from the beginning inseparably part of him, as his refusal to go to school—that is, to start on social life—without her bears out (ll.15-24). Their separation illustrates that a sense of separateness and social obstacles will have to be overcome before a full union can be achieved. The hero will have to learn, will have to gain wider experience, before the union can become socially relevant. Yet in the end Blauncheflour is still the ideal young love who literally forgets the whole world—the necessity to keep up her duties towards the Emir—when she is with her lover (ll.979-1039). Also ideally, she had remained absolutely faithful to Floris, to the point of contemplating suicide rather than being another man's wife (ll.907-20).

Further details of his experience of woman Floris encounters in his mother. On the one hand she shares with Blauncheflour's mother a 'malevolent' role in maintaining the falsehood of the girl's death, which provides Floris with a reason to leave her as well as his father. But on the other hand Floris' mother is a manifestation of the virtue of love. Her role is to civilize her husband and their relationship with their child, thereby setting their son free to start out on his own. Thus to the hero's experience and to the story's scope she adds the fundamental notion that love is an ennobling force and that it can overcome all obstacles in its way.

Blauncheflour's friend and confidante Clarice adds to Floris' experience a woman's capacity for devoted loyalty, as also for clever subterfuge, when she tells the Emir that Blauncheflour slept late because she had been praying for him all night (ll.1005-14). She parallels Floris' mother, who also risked displeasure and resorted to subterfuge—the suggestion to sell Blauncheflour away and simulate her death was hers— to achieve what she held to be a more civilized order of affairs. There is, therefore, poetic justice in Clarice being married to the Emir, another uncouth husband whom, no doubt, she is to civilize, thus creating a neat end to this story of integrity. The formal pattern of ennobling love thus reigns supreme, against all improbabilities.

The other characters in *Fl & Bl* are devices to help enact the above pattern. The good men and women along the road serve as guides to Floris on his way to private happiness which is the social good. The gatekeeper's opposite number on the right side, Daris, is the clearest example of the disinterested guide, who has nothing to gain but the common good, which in terms of this romance is Floris' union with Blauncheflour.

The frequency of this guidance may be worth notice. Three times Floris receives information and guidance on the road: first from a land-lady (ll.428-39), then from the men of Babylon, the 'talk of the town' (ll.465-76), and finally again from a landlord, another member of that life-sustaining and rest-providing guild (ll.527-36). Then he is three times passed on into other hands, by his last host to Daris (ll.549-58), by Daris to the gatekeeper (ll.607-818), and by the gatekeeper to Clarice (ll.850-68). In the meantime Floris has used three disguises: that of a merchant (l.370), that of an engineer or builder (ll.748-50), and that of a 'flower' in a basket of flowers (l.854). Rather than tracing 'magic' or 'fertility' or other symbolic origins for the number three, it is helpful to realize that in children's games and in play between grown-up and child such generally agreed numbers—usually three or a hundred—serve as suspense-building devices. Whether or not the number three has conno-tations of perfect harmony, the repetition certainly has a formal function. On the symbolic level it may point to integrity to be gained, but as a for-mal pattern it is also a suspense-building device, in the same way that, later on, the introduction of the Emir's chamberlain and the calling in of the barons near the end are suspense-building devices.

Because it is not the individual characters but the whole action that represents human experience in this type of story, the setting and the 'stage properties' must also be considered as part of the experience.

Fl & Bl appears to progress by means of situations and objects of an archetypal nature. The archetypal situations of a young lover's conflicts with father and rivals and his experience with women and guides have been sketched above.[2] Of archetypal 'props' the most outstanding are the tomb, the ring, the precious stones, the chalices or cups, and the flowers. In this formal type of story these 'props' are to be read as symbolic agents in the total experience.

The recurrent symbols marking the progress of *Fl & Bl* are the cup and the ring. It is typical of this story that the progress should be marked by female symbols rather than male ones such as swords and lances. There is no mention of weapons, as there is no fighting, chivalric or oth-

---

[2] For a further discussion along Jungian lines, see Reiss, 1971:339-50.

erwise. The love idealism portrayed in *Fl & Bl* concentrates on the ado-
lescent hero's quest for integration of the feminine aspects of life,
excluding the simultaneous development of the masculine aspects.

The cup appears in two forms. The cup that was given in payment
for Blauncheflour (ll.161-82) is central. Instead of the girl herself, a
symbol of her remains behind. Floris would not be 'alive' without her
presence, even if only in a symbolic form. Therefore, when he sets out to
be reunited with Blauncheflour, that *ilke self coupe* ('very same cup',
l.373) is given to him by his father because *Herewiþ þou may þat swete
þing / Wynne* ('with this you can win back that sweet girl', ll.376-77).
The cup points out the purpose of Floris' quest and does turn out to be the
key that opens the gate to the girl. It is the right equipment to gain
admittance, and therefore convinces the gatekeeper (ll.781-822).

So, by staying behind, the cup shows the hero what he must go in
search of if he is to be re-integrated. As long as that has not been
achieved, Floris is not really 'alive', which is illustrated by the fact that he
goes without food because he misses her (ll.129-30; 417-18; 493-94; 577-
83). Characteristically, when he receives information about
Blauncheflour, he rewards his guides with cups (ll.444-48; 517-22).
These other cups emphasize the role of the first cup as pointer: Floris can
symbolically give his cup away in exchange for directions towards
Blauncheflour. When he comes to her actual gatekeeper, he does so literally.

The ring, which in psychology as in alchemy not only symbolizes
the female but also truth (since it has neither beginning nor end), operates
on both these symbolic levels. When Floris has reached the point when he
can set out to win his love, it is given to him—typically—by his mother.

> Haue nou, sone, here þis ring;
> While þou hit hast, doute þe no þing,
> Ne fir þe brenne, ne drenchen in se,
> Ne iren ne stel schal derie þe;
> And be hit erli and be hit late,
> To þi wille þou schalt haue whate.
>   (ll.391-96)

(Now, my sone, take this ring. Be not afraid of anything as long as you pos-
sess it: no fire shall burn you, you shall not drown in the sea. Neither iron nor

steel shall harm you. And whether early or late, you shall have the wherewithal to satisfy your wants.)

This incantation-like speech indicates that now, when he has shown himself independent enough to set out, he can wear this ring which, like the cup, adds the feminine aspect to his male personality, thus making him whole. And with that integrity he shall be safe against the elements, which are hostile to him as long as he has not achieved integration, as his mother's words imply: against the fire, the water and the iron that can kill him. And the sustaining earth shall not fail him.

Parallel to this, another ring is given to Floris by his last host on the way, to be given to Daris (ll.555-58). This ring also protects him, here from the effects of being a stranger, and it serves to identify him to his next and most essential guide. This ring tells Daris the truth about Floris the lover. And telling the truth about Floris and Blauncheflour is also what the first ring ultimately does (ll.1149ff). Its protective power is again hinted at: *þou ne schalt nowt die whiles hit is þin* ('you shall not die as long as it is yours, l.1152). But its protective effect is shown to consist in its showing the truth of the great—because essential—love between the two. It is not its magic but its symbolism that is effective. It is the fact that both insist on the other's wearing it, sacrificing their own lives for the sake of the other, that convinces the Emir that this is a true love that he must not destroy.

The quest for Blauncheflour is a quest from death to life. Their union is life in social terms; their separation is death, as the tomb scene emphasizes. At Blauncheflour's supposed tomb Floris realizes that for him by himself there is no life. So he decides to commit suicide (ll.301-12). This scene illustrates that parental restraint, when pushed to the absolute, is death for the child. The child must be able to get out on its own, in order to achieve an identity and a place of its own in the whole. Floris' identity threatens to be killed until, as I said above, his mother gives life to him again by preventing his suicide.

Also Floris' swooning on various occasions suggests that apparently insuperable obstacles to his reunion mean for him the loss of his identity—here symbolized as consciousness. He swoons for the first time when he hears from her mother that Blauncheflour is dead (l.246), and three times, so more absolutely, when he is reading the inscription on her tomb (l.267). And he is once more to swoon three times when he has heard how absolutely inaccessible Blauncheflour is in the Emir's power.

Having progressed 'through' the tomb, Floris begins to show— temporary—signs of independence: *Now, moder, y þink þat y leve may* ('Mother, I believe that I can leave now', 1.341). And he even takes command: *"Leue fader," he seide, "y telle þe / Al þat þou shalt fynde me"* ('"Dear father," he said, "I shall name you all that you must provide me with"' (ll.355-56). But his initiation to life is by no means complete. He has so far only been initiated into the quest stage. His approach to union is marked by obstacles, as if it consists of so many stages. Each of these obstacles is of a kind that could have symbolic power, but this does not appear to be worked out in this rendering of the tale. The first obstacle after the tomb is water, the *salte flod* that he must cross (1.455). It marks the beginning of the Babylon stage. The second obstacle is a bridge (ll.549-52), at the end of which he shall find his most essential guide Daris. This bridge he 'achieves' by means of the above-mentioned second ring. Between his guide and his goal is the third obstacle, the city-wall of Babylon and its defending knights (ll.608-34). And ultimately there is the tower with its eunuchs and gatekeeper (ll.635-78).

With the tower in Babylon the obstacles do acquire symbolic power: *And in þe bourh, amide þeri3t / þer stant a riche tour, I þe aply3t* ('and in the city, right in the middle, there stands a rich tower, I assure you', ll.635-36). The tower in its setting of Babylon or the orchard almost suggests a *mandala*: it possesses a number of the perennial symbols of the achievement of inner wholeness. It is crowned with a sun-like jewel (ll.655-60) and it is presented as a place of bliss:

> So wel were þat ilke man
> Þat mi3te wonen in þat an,
> Nou þourt him neuere, ful iwis,
> Willen after more blisse.
>   (ll.663-66)

(Any man who would be able to live in it would be fortunate to such a degree that he need not, indeed, ever wish for greater happiness.)

The description of the Emir's orchard adds to the symbolic power of the setting in which Blauncheflour is found. The description of Paradise in the *Book of Genesis*, and most especially in Milton's *Paradise Lost*, Book IV, as also the description of the Garden in the *Roman de la Rose*, show that a setting of the Tree of Love and/or a Tree of Life and a fountain and flowers, birds and precious stones is felt to be the appropriate one for love and integrity. The Emir's *locus amoenus* likewise has birds (1.691), precious stones (ll.693-96 and 701-03), a well from Paradise (ll.697-700), a Tree of Love (ll.721-23) and flowers (ll.724-26).

In *Fl & Bl* it is, and at the same time is not, the place of reunion of the lovers. Tower and orchard suggest that this is the final place where the quest finds its fulfilment. The object of the quest, Blauncheflour, is there in the appropriate setting for what she is for Floris. That this 'enemy territory' presents itself primarily, in its imagery, as the place of achievement of the desired object, must be understood in the light of the fact that in this type of story every element is to be seen in relation to the protagonist. Inner wholeness is to be achieved there, so the setting suggests. But the final achievement contains in itself also the final test.The place constitutes, at the same time, a major danger from which Floris must rescue Blauncheflour and himself: a paradise—symbol of social achievement—manipulated by the false values of the Emir, whose abominable fertility-cult of mating for the season is a perversion of the perfect love that the romance seeks: a fully integrated social ideal, based on loyalty instead of manipulation and on love instead of mere pleasure.

But Floris is not yet ready to achieve this rescue. First he must pass the Cerberus-gatekeeper into the underworld of a symbolic death, to rise to life again in his proper form in the basket of flowers. The gatekeeper first appears as another peacock-rival or obstacle to Floris' achievement of love, prefiguring one aspect of the Emir (ll.679-80), but in the detailed instructions that follow he is presented as a Cerberus controlling the entrance to the Paradise of Blauncheflour's setting. Like the porter to the Underworld of Greek mythology he is said to rob the applicant of his possessions: *He wille him bo þe bete and reue* ('he will beat as well as rob him', 1.678). He is wary of people who are just curious:

> Wel sone he wil come to þe
> And aske what mister man þou be
> And ber vpon þe felonie,
> And saie þou art comen þe tour aspie.
> > (ll.753-56; see above for translation)

Serious applicants for entrance he submits to the test of the game of chess, by which they must pay for his services in conducting them in.

The game of chess (ll.764-814) is traditionally an initiation
through symbolic death and rebirth. Floris' boyish dependence on others
will have to die, so that he shall be reborn as a man able to play his own
game. The gatekeeper shall not be his guide, but his servant. How much
effort this developemnt takes, what price Floris must pay, is indicated by
the three stages that the game takes, with doubled and tripled stakes and
finally by the sacrifice of the cup itself which symbolizes Floris' life, as I
have argued above.

After this Cerberus' assistance—the first integration or loyalty—
has been secured by Floris' symbolic death, the seed of the new hero is
buried in the coffin of the basket, from which the flower Floris will
resurrect. Dramatizing the continual risk to which the ideal is exposed, he
is carried to the 'wrong' place, so that his resurrection might yet prove
death, acted out as Floris' diving back into the basket again (ll.861-78).
But the girl Clarice, to whose room he has been carrried, 'revives' him,
thus prefiguring an aspect of Blauncheflour. She shows a further integration, now of a woman's capacity for fellow-feeling, healing and ten-
der care:

> 'Ne doute ȝou nammore wiþalle
> Þan to miself hit hadde bifalle.
> Wite ȝe wel witerli
> Þat hele ich wille ȝoure boþer druri.'
> To on bedde ȝhe haþ hem ibrowt
> Þat was of silk and sendal wrout.
> Þai sette hem þere wel softe adoun,
> And Clarice drowȝ þe courtyn roun.
>   (ll.953-60)

('Be no more afraid in this matter than if it had happened to me. You may rest
assured that I will keep the love between the two of you a secret.' She took
them to a bed that was made with silk and sendal. They lay down in it very
comfortably and Clarice drew the curtain round them.)

Now Floris and Blauncheflour are finally reunited, but their quest
has not yet come to an end. Their place in the whole of society they still
have to win. The parental and jealous rival figure of the Emir demands
final proof of their love. A last initiation awaits them. Their enclosure in
a dungeon (l.1088) symbolizes that they must die again, now together.

But they only achieve their ultimate initiation by voluntarily accepting literal death, the one sacrificing himself or herself for the other. This scene of their mutually taking the blame and of the insistent exchanging of the protective ring (ll.1135-82), followed by their taking each other's place under the Emir's sword (ll.1193-1230), reveals their full beauty, the glory of their true love, for all to see.

In *Fl & Bl*, then, we have indulged the fancy and we have heard of love, in that order. How perennial this experience is, every lover of Mozart's *The Magic Flute* will recognize. The Middle English *Fl & Bl* has rendered the experiences simply and briskly. The rich archetypal suggestiveness does not clog the pure and direct manner of the narrative. What Atkins referred to as a "good tale" turns out to be a well-structured tale: without the support of any extensive discussion or moral, the carefully handled formal and symbolic patterns bring out the significance of the tale in the most immediate manner.

REFERENCES

Atkins, J.W.H. (1907). Metrical Romances, 1200-1500. II. In: *The Cambridge History of English Literature*. Ed. A.W. Ward and A.R. Waller. Vol. I. Cambridge: C.U.P. 301-19.
Reiss, E. (1971). Symbolic Detail in Medieval Narrative: *Floris and Blancheflour*. *Papers in Language and Literature* 7. 339-50.
Stevens, J. (1973). *Medieval Romance: Themes and Approaches*. London: Hutchinson.
Taylor, A.B. (ed.) (1927). *Floris and Blaunchefbour: A Middle English Romance. Edited from the Trentham and Auchinleck MSS*. Oxford: O.U.P.

DAME SIRITH AND *DE CLERICO ET PUELLA*

KEITH BUSBY
(University of Leiden)

A good deal of Middle English literature is derived either directly or indirectly from Old French. Genres that make their first appearance on the continent (or in England in French-speaking circles) are later taken over by authors writing in English. The French influence on Middle English literature is almost incalculable, as it is both pervasive and persistent, and assumes many forms. The most evident of these forms is, of course, the translation from French into English, but instances of literal translation from one language into another are rare in the Middle Ages in general. Whilst there are many cases of what look like translations, closer examination reveals that they are actually adaptations: English poets working with a French text in front of them tailor it to fit the tastes and requirements of a new and different audience.

Whilst the narrative line of, say, Chrétien de Troyes's Arthurian romance *Yvain* (*Le Chevalier au Lion*) remains intact in the adaptation, the essence of the poem does not.Chrétien's original aristocratic audience appreciated the finer points of courtly, chivalric, and amorous behaviour, and took great pleasure in listening to detailed and often rhetorical analysis of sentiment; the Middle English *Ywain and Gawain*, on the other hand, seems to have been destined for a public of fourteenth-century *nouveaux riches* who did not apparently appreciate this aspect of Chrétien's poem, and the English version is consequently transformed from a courtly romance into a fast-moving story of adventure. Another type of work that shows the profound influence of French literature on English is original English works written with a detailed knowledge of French texts and constituting in some ways responses to them. Staying with Arthurian romance for the moment, the best example is probably *Sir Gawain and the Green Knight*, a poem for which no French model exists, but which shows indisputable knowledge (and understanding) of the French tradition. Although inconceivable without the French Gauvain, the English Gawain is very English indeed. On a more general level, themes, modes, images, styles of writing that developed first in French are taken up later and anglicized. Without the model of French, English medieval literature would have been very different.

It may seem rather odd to have started this chapter, which deals with *Dame Sirith* and *De Clerico et Puella*, by mentioning two Arthurian romances, which are at first sight unrelated to our texts. However, whereas Middle English literature of the fourteenth century, generally speaking, reflects in its own way the constitution of the corpus of French, there are some types of literature that are notable for their scarcity in Middle English, although they abound in French. One of these is the *fabliau*, of which *Dame Sirith* is the only undisputed example outside of Chaucer's works; whilst *De Clerico* cannot be called a *fabliau* proper, it is clearly related to the genre (I shall return to this in my brief discussion of the poem towards the end of this paper). In my opinion, the absence of *fabliaux* in Middle English is intimately linked to both the nature of romance and the language situation in the British Isles in the Middle Ages.

First, however, a word about *fabliaux* in general. The word *fabliau* is a Picard (North-Eastern) dialect form of *fableau* (also attested), derived from Latin *fabulellum*, a diminutive of *fabula*. Without going into the detailed historical semantics of these words, the Old French word *fableau/fabliau* means literally 'little story, little fiction'. Scholars use the Picard form to designate the genre because it seems to have flourished in North-Eastern France more than in other regions, and this in the thirteenth and fourteenth centuries. There have been many attempts to define the *fabliau*, most of them unsatisfactory in one way or another, and indeed, the matter is one of the most notorious problems of French literary scholarship. The attempts clearly fail because the poems regarded as *fabliaux* are many and varied, and resist strict categorisation. Moreover, the modern mania for definitions almost certainly does not correspond to the medieval view of literature. In fact, the only "definition" that has won currency in scholarly circles is an extremely loose one formulated by the great French scholar Joseph Bédier as early as 1894: "les fabliaux sont des contes à rire en vers" ('the fabliaux are comic tales in verse'). The obvious reservationsthat have to be made about this phrase are that there are other comic tales in verse not generally regarded as *fabliaux* and that some poems generally accepted to be *fabliaux* are not very humorous, at least not to our eyes. Rather than become involved here in the hornet's nest of genre-definitions and related problems, I shall give a brief *description*, not *definition*, of the *fabliaux*.

The *fabliaux* vary in length from about fifty to over one thousand lines and are almost without exception written in octosyllabic rhyming couplets. They treat a wide variety of subjects, but are frequently—but not exclusively—concerned with what we sometimes call "low" life. The *fabliaux* are usually set in a rural or urban (but not normally aristocratic) setting, and the characters are peasants, merchants, their wives, and priests or monks; the nobility appear only infrequently, but their appearance is not insignificant. In *fabliaux*, we may see the parish priest making love with the baker's wife and being castrated as punishment; we may see examples of native peasant cunning, which nearly all involve practical jokes; sex, food, and excrement also feature widely in the *fabliaux*, and there are few subjects that are taboo.Common to most of the *fabliaux* is the idea of ruse and deception, and the plot of many of them revolves around some form of trick. In keeping with the setting and subject-matter, the style of the *fabliaux* is frequently less courtly than, say, that of the romance, but there are notable exceptions.

It is not difficult to understand, in the light of this brief description, why the *fabliaux* were for many years considered to be the bourgeois or peasant counterpart to courtly literature. After all, the subjects are usually far from courtly, and much closer to the world of the bourgeoisie and peasantry than to that of the aristocracy. Yet, when the matter is considered logically, considerable problems arise. Are merchants and peasants likely to enjoy literature in which their peers without exception are made to look foolish? How do we explain the presence of *fabliaux* in the same manuscripts as religious poems, romances, and other forms of courtly literature? We are, of course, dealing with what is probably the most difficult of all issues that confront the medieval literary scholar, that of the intended audience of the literature.

The question of the audience of *fabliaux* used until fairly recently to be discussed in terms of clear-cut social categories: either they were meant for the bourgeoisie (Bédier's thesis) or they were intended for the aristocracy (Per Nykrog's thesis of 1957). Whilst Bédier's assumption was based on the subject-matter (non-courtly for a non-courtly audience), Nykrog's took as its point of departure the presence of parody. There is a good deal of parody in the *fabliaux*, notably of courtly literature, and parody is ineffective unless the audience appreciates ,what is being parodied. *Ergo*, since the *fabliaux* parody courtly literature, they must share the same audience. There can be no denying the validity of this thesis: some *fabliaux* are even built up of themes and narrative elements proper to the courtly romance; some contain specific allusions to, even quotations from, courtly texts.

It hardly needs to be said that the truth is more complicated, and that the one theory does not necessarily exclude the other, for whilst courtly literature may, initially at least, have been intended exclusively for the nobility, there is no reason to believe that the *fabliaux* were as socially confined as romance. Indeed, their nature is such that they must have appealed to many different kinds of medieval people. In what is probably the most sophisticated and tolerant discussion to date of *fabliaux* audiences, Jean Rychner has shown how different versions of the same poem can be explained as adaptations for audiences with a different make-up. Thus, a *fabliau* with elements of courtly parody may be rewritten for a non-courtly audience, the courtly allusions, etc., being omitted since they would not be appreciated. The process may also take place in the other direction. On the other hand, the non-courtly audience could have appreciated the basic humour of a tale as it was, even though the parody was beyond them, and there was nothing to stop a sophisticated courtly audience having a belly-laugh at a poem which contained no courtly parody. We are probably much nearer the truth if we think of a heterogeneous audience containing people from all walks of life, rather than a homogeneous one made up of *either* the aristocracy *or* the bourgeoisie *and/or* the peasantry.

By and large, it does not seem to me that there is any real reason for not actually considering the *fabliaux* as part and parcel of courtly literature, particularly in view of their manuscript context mentioned above. In this respect, then, and by virtue of their relationship to the kind of literature they parody, the *fabliaux* partly owe their existence to romance, upon which they offer a kind of down-to-earth commentary. This can be seen as one of the reasons for the curious lack of *fabliaux* in Middle English, for the kind of elements of courtly literature that are parodied (the love interest, the finer points of courtly and chivalric behaviour, etc.) are generally the aspects that receive less attention in Middle English romance as a whole. Thus, since the object of the parody does not exist in English romance, one of the *raisons d' être* of the French *fabliau* is not operative in the English situation.

The other major reason for the paucity of *fabliaux* in English has to do with linguistic conditions. For a good part of the Middle Ages, French was the language of the majority of the aristocracy in England, and thus of literature. The consequence is that most Old French literature was comprehensible to English audiences for the twelfth and thirteenth centuries and much of the fourteenth. The French *fabliaux* almost certainly circulated in England, and indeed, a number of them are written in Anglo-Norman, the insular dialect of French spoken and written by the Norman rulers of England. It is therefore not necessary to speak of the English *fabliaux* as forming part of a vast "lost literature of medieval England", or to speculate that the English did not share the *esprit gaulois* of the French and their taste for the scurrilous and bawdy. It is fair to conclude that there was little need for *fabliaux* in Middle English for most of the Middle Ages, as they were regarded as a type of poem better suited to expression in French. Similar arguments can be brought to bear as an explanation for the equally curious lack of animal epic (*Roman de Renart*) or animal fable in Middle English, represented outside of Chaucer's works only by *The Fox and the Wolf* (found in the same manuscript as *Dame Sirith*).

As for Chaucer, he is, as usual, a remarkable exception to the rule. *The Canterbury Tales* contain a number of *fabliaux* (the most celebrated of which are no doubt *The Miller's Tale* and *The Reeve's Tale*) and an animal fable (*The Nun's Priest's Tale*). It has been suggested that one of Chaucer's aims in *The Canterbury Tales* was to give a survey of the different types of narrative genre current in his time. Since Chaucer is thoroughly Gallicised (but in a very English way), it is not surprising to find his narrative universe containing examples of the *fabliau* and the animal fable, for they also respond to the more courtly tales in the collection. *The Miller's Tale* is both a general and a specific reaction to *The Knight's Tale*: it is *fabliau* responding to romance; it is told by the drunken miller in an attempt to "quite" the Knight; it is also concerned with the rivalry of two men for one woman ..., etc. *The Miller's Tale* exploits the potential of the *fabliaux* as no French poem does, and *The Nun's Priest's Tale*, whilst clearly an animal fable, exceeds its French models, with the possible exception of *Isopet*, by exploring in the most absurd fashion the theme of the power of rhetoric.

Dame Sirith and the Weeping Bitch is thus something of an oddity
in Middle English, and perhaps all the more interesting because of that. I
have already mentioned that it is contained in the same manuscript as *The
Fox and the Wolf*, and this is probably not a coincidence. MS. Digby 86
of the Bodleian Library in Oxford is an anthology of pieces in verse and
prose in Middle English, Anglo-Norman, and Latin. There are a number
of manuscripts like it, the most famous of which is probably the precious
MS. Harley 2253 of the British Library, a comparable but not identical
collection. The compiler of Digby 86, a relatively early manuscript,
shows signs of a desire to be fashionable, and the presence of the *fabliau*
of *Dame Sirith* and the animal fable of *The Fox and the Wolf* can therefore be attributed to this desire. In addition, he also seems to have had a
predilection for particularly scurrilous poetry, as he has also included the
Anglo-Norman *Lai du Cor* (a chastity-test that takes place at Arthur's
court) and one of the most disgusting French *fabliaux*, *Les Quatre
Souhaits Saint Martin*, scarcely repeatable even in summary.
     This is not the place to explore in detail the analogues to *Dame
Sirith* and to discuss the relationships between them. Suffice it to say here
that there are plenty of similar stories, not only in the corpus of French
fabliaux, but also in Oriental story collections. This need not astonish us,
for the nature of the *fabliau* plot in general is such that folklorists can
provide us with interesting material for comparison. We should not,
however, make the mistake of regarding *fabliaux* as traditional folktale,
for some of them are very sophisticated literary productions, despite
their frequently scurrilous subject-matter.
     The Anglo-Norman heading in the manuscript suggests what kind
of a poem *Dame Sirith* is: it is a *fablel* (a variant of *fabliau*) concerned
with the *cointise* of Dame Sirith. *Cointise* is a word with many meanings
in Old French, but here it clearly indicates something like "cleverness,
ingenuity", leading the audience to believe that this is the main subject of
the poem. Indeed, after we have read or listened to *Dame Sirith*, what
remains in our mind is not the love of Willikin for Margery, but the trick
by means of which Dame Sirith brings about their union.
     The poem opens in a traditional "minstrel" manner, with an
announcement of the source (ll.1-2) and then the subject (ll.3-15). It is
therefore already evident that the poem is going to be concerned with the
lover's attempts to win the lady. The style of the opening is also typical of
certain other Middle English poems, with ll.4-6 in particular recalling

the romance tradition by virtue of their use of short alliterative formulae. The social setting of the poem is also indicated by the mention of the husband's profession (1.18); he is a merchant, so this is to be no poem of courtly love between knights and ladies. Still the alliterative formulae pile up (ll.21, 23).

Starting with 1.25, the poem makes full use of dialogue, even to the extent of making itself susceptible of performance; it is not difficult to imagine how a talented *jongleur* or minstrel could have exploited the dialogue, changing voices (and possibly even hats) as the speech alternated from one character to another. The merchant's wife is the object of the as yet unnamed protagonist's affections, as had already been indicated in 1.20. In the light of his imminent amorous confession, her offer to do anything he desires (ll.29-36) acquires in retrospect an ironic tinge, and is obviously not meant by her to be taken absolutely literally. The direct and sudden declaration of love that follows (ll.67 ff.) is in itself interesting: had this been a courtly poem, the characters would no doubt have been shown suffering torments of love and analysing their sentiments in great rhetorical detail before stammering out a bashful declaration. Whilst the poet had said in 1.9 that the lover *heuede wrong* (probably 'suffered anguish or pain', rather than 'committed a sin'), there is not much timidity about him. The declaration is preceded by a repeated statement of a "courtly" desire not to offend her in any way (ll.38-39, 41-42). The whole scene itself invites comparison with Nicholas's first approach to Alison in Chaucer's *The Miller's Tale*.

The courtly influence becomes steadily more apparent in the lady's reply to the as yet unspecified request: *houncurteis* (1.46) and *vilte* (1.47) are both words of French origin and belong to romance and lyric poetry. The humour of this passage lies, as I have suggested, in her suggestion that she will accede to his request, providing she does not incur shame; the eventual granting or denial of her love she makes dependent on his eloquence and persuasiveness (ll.52-53). Furthermore, her assurance that she will not blame him for whatever he might say seems to relieve him of any tension and enables him to express himself freely. He has won himself a fair hearing and so cannot grumble (ll.58-60). Interestingly, he calls the lady's response to his request *hende* (1.61), which is one of the Middle English words used alongside *curteis* and *fre* (cf. 1.34) to denote 'courteous' or 'courtly'.

The lover now makes his true confession (ll.66 ff.): he has loved her for many years, but was afraid to visit her while her husband was in town. The absence of the husband to visit the fair in Boston is at the same time a narrative device common in *fabliaux* (which makes the lover's visit possible) and a method of locating the action in a typically provincial setting (French *fabliaux* are rarely set in Paris, but rather in Normandy, Abbeville, Arras, etc.). The implied possessiveness (ll.70-73, 82-84) of the husband also marks him as a *mari jaloux*, possibly even a *senex amans* ('old lover'), one of the stereotypes not only of the *fabliaux* but also of such courtly literature as the *Lais* of Marie de France or a good proportion of the courtly lyric in both Provençal and French. The lover's speech switches constantly in tone from the non-courtly (the invitation to bed, your husband has gone to Boston, etc.) to the courtly (do not be offended, you speak courteously, etc.), and ll.85-87 are the words and sentiment of the typical courtly lover: "Lady, if it is your will, I will love you secretly and silently." Secrecy is indeed one of the notable characteristics of that variety of love that critics have often called, in the wake of Gaston Paris and C.S. Lewis, *amour courtois* or *courtly love*, and which I have myself alluded to earlier. Whilst we must bear in mind that courtly love is an invention of modern scholars and that we should not expect to find the "classic" variety (eventual adultery between beseeching lover and pitiless lady of higher social class, secrecy, suffering, refined analysis of sentiment, etc.) in every or even any single text, it is still a handy concept if used cautiously.

The lady's reaction to this confession is disappointing, especially in the light of her earlier hint of readiness to oblige: she indignantly invokes the holy sacrament of marriage, the duty of wife to husband (*louerd* and *spouse*, 1.91), and the strength of the love between them. Nor does she wish to soil her reputation as an honest woman; the indignant and proper tone of the rebuke is vitiated somewhat by 1.102, where she specifies precisely where she will not *don selk falsete*. The lover's disappointment is evident, but he does not give up hope, reminding her once more of her *curteisi* (1.110), and hoping that God will change her mind (just as she had earlier called on Him whilst expressing the opposite sentiment). The lady's next speech is another mixture of the courtly and the non-courtly. She begins by asking whether he takes her for a fool, and then questions his sanity in no uncertain terms (ll.115-17). The description of her husband (ll.119-20) is couched in the purest courtly language (*curteis, hende, pris* [another French word]), and she once more stresses her own wifely virtue and honour (ll.121-26). Again, the lover's reaction is traditional and courtly: *Swete lemmon* (l.127) is the standard mode of address of lover to lady in Middle English love poetry; *vilani* (l.128) is another French word belonging to the vocabulary of love; the importance of the secrecy of the love is repeated (l.130); *won* ("happiness", l.132) seems to be the equivalent of the *joi* of Troubadour lyric poetry, which often stands for the successful culmination of the lover's suit in sexual and spiritual union.

The lover's departure is again characteristic: the lady is pitiless, even sarcastic (ll.134-35), in her rejection, bringing very much to mind the *Belle Dame sans Merci* of courtly lyric and romance. And the lover, repeating helplessly the lady's remark about wasting his time and effort (ll.134, 140-41), and indulging in self-pity but not giving up hope (for a courtly lover never does), leaves with another appeal to Heaven to make his beloved change her mind.

This constitutes the end of the first section of the narrative, and leads into the lover's first meeting with the go-between, Dame Sirith. The go-between is a common figure in literature in general, and particularly common in the *fabliaux* (for obvious reasons), whilst not altogether absent from romance (one thinks notably of the servant-girl Lunete in Chrétien de Troyes's *Yvain*). Although the lover is *drerimod* (l.149) and generally depressed, he is not entirely at his wit's end, retaining a fair level of self-composure, enough in any case to offer Dame Sirith (note that she is also, ironically, called *hende* in l.154) money in return for her services. In a sense, the encounter between the lover and Dame Sirith is a structural variation on his meeting with the lady (now reavealed as *Margeri*, l.177). He requests her for help, without specifying its precise nature (ll.161-66); she expresses willingness to co-operate and asks for further details (ll.167-72); in his reply he assumes once more the role and tone of the rebuffed courtly lover, even going so far as to suggest that he may commit suicide unless the lady changes her mind (ll.173-84). Dame Sirith's secondary response is, like the lady's, indignant, and she appeals to God, claiming that acceding to his request would entail loss of virtue and would bring shame on herself. In fact, her greatest concern is to rid herself of the suspicion of witchcraft (certainly not hinted at in the text). The combination of the lover's reassurance and the offer of money and clothing begins to change her mind.

Dame Sirith is also concerned that her client (now called *Wilekin*, l.229) really does love Margery (ll.229-31), and especially that he intends to keep the affair secret, for otherwise she runs the risk of being accused of complicity in an immoral act and actually being taken to court (1.244). Here, an aspect of the traditional courtly love affair, the secrecy, is presented in what is effectively another mode: until now, it had been put only by Willikin as *dernelike* (1.86) and *derne loue* (1.130), both conventional phrases; now the secrecy is important for practical reasons to an old woman afraid of legal prosecution. With Willikin's repeated assurance of his good intentions, the scene is now set for Dame Sirith's contribution, and the audience now turn their attention to exactly how this old lady with a reputation for cunning is going to persuade Margery to grant her favours to Willikin. There is little doubt at this point that Willikin will succeed: from a narrative point of view, the problem and situation are evident, and all the ingredients necessary for the resolution are present. We are therefore now concerned with *how*, not *whether*, things will work out.

It is true that Dame Sirith herself almost suggests that she is about to practice some form of magic in order to achieve her ends (ll.264-66, 276-78), but Willikin's offer of twenty pounds for her trouble reduces the affair to a more mercenary level. The poet maintains suspense, for even after Dame Sirith's saying she will give pepper, mustard and vinegar to the dog (ll.279-81), and Willikin's sceptical, not to say incomprehending, reaction, the audience is still in the dark as to exactly what her plans are. We know no more than Willikin at this point: simply that she will *make a lesing* (1.282) of some kind. Dame Sirith also refers to the ruse she is planning as a *gin* (1.289), derived from Old French *engin*, one of the words commonly used to describe a trick in the *fabliaux*. Willikin is to wait until Dame Sirith returns from her visit to Margery.

The suspense is kept up as Dame Sirith goes to Margery's house and laments loudly about her pitiable state (ll.297-314). Margery falls for the deception, invites her in and offers to feed her (ll.315-30). Note the narrator's comment on Dame Sirith, *Christ awarie hire lif!* (1.332: 'May Christ damn her way of life!'), which is tantamount to approval of whatever it is she is about to do. The old woman then begins a tale about her married daughter being courted by a clerk (ll.338 ff.) which bears a not entirely coincidental relationship to the story of Willikin's frustrated courtship of Margery. It is at this point, when we see the parallel between the two tales, that we begin to get some intimation of what she is up to, especially when she says that the clerk in love with her daughter has turned her into a bitch because she did not return his love. Her pointing to the dog, weeping, of course, because of the pepper, mustard and vinegar, is the narrative equivalent of the conjuror's pulling a rabbit out of the hat (ll.335ff). From the particular case of her daughter, she draws a general conclusion (ll.361-64) which has the desired effect on Margery, now terrified that Willikin will bewitch her, too (ll.365-70).

Dame Sirith's *gin* has worked, to Willikin's benefit, we may now confidently assume, and doubly to her own, for not only does she stand to receive Willikin's money but Margery's gifts as well (ll.388-90). *Dame Sirith* now ends swiftly and predictably, for once the old woman's ingenuity has been revealed and admired, the poet realises as a good storyteller that there is little point in prolonging his tale. Willikin is about to achieve his desire, though not because Margery has changed her feelings towards him, despite her apparent recapitulation in ll.425-32. There is a cynical contrast between Margery's motivation (fear of being turned into a dog) and the terms in which she offers herself to Willikin, which are those of the courtly lover. This type of love-language we have noticed earlier in the poem, but this is really the first time it has been used by Margery. Dame Sirith's own final speech, the last of the poem as a whole, is equally cynical. It is clear, first of all, exactly what love means to her (ll.440-41) and exactly what she expects Willikin to get up to as soon as she has left; secondly, her parting words, addressed to the audience as much as the other characters, amount to a kind of professional statement on her own behalf and that of other go-betweens.

The *Interludium de Clerico et Puella* is a slighter piece than *Dame Sirith*. It is important, however, for the history of English drama, although it is probably something of an exaggeration to call it the oldest secular play extant in English. In fact, like *Dame Sirith*, it may well have been intended for recitation by a single *jongleur* or minstrel rather than for a "theatrical" performance by a number of actors. Its treatment of basically the same theme as *Dame Sirith* is more economical and arguably more immediate and dramatic. Because of its brevity, its author does not have the time to employ the stylistic and narrative devices that make *Dame Sirith* what it is, but there are remarkable resemblances between the two poems. These can be found not only on the plot level (it is likely that *De Clerico* would have been a complete analogue to *Dame Sirith*, had it been preserved fully), but also on the verbal and stylistic (some of these are given by Bennett and Smithers, p.372). Whilst the influence of the courtly style is less evident in *De Clerico*, it is not entirely lacking (cf. the clerk's lament in ll.17-26, and the use of romance loanwords such as *clerc fayllard* [l.8], *trua* [l.35], *cunsayle* [l.54]). However, given the nature of both pieces and their relationship to the *fabliau* tradition, there seems little point in attempting to establish a direct link between the two: while we cannot rule out the possibility that the one is an abbreviated or expanded version of the other, it is more likely that they are simply two out of many versions of the story that may have once existed. In its verse-form, *De Clerico* is closer than most of *Dame Sirith* to the Old French *fabliau*: whilst it is not written in octosyllabic couplets, *De Clerico* shows rhyming couplets with four beats which approximate to the French form. Scholars have yet to provide a satisfactory explanation for the alternating verse patterns in *Dame Sirith*.

Dame Sirith and *De Clerico et Puella* prove, if proof were required, that English poetry before Chaucer is not lacking in humour. One of the major issues of *fabliau* scholarship used to be that of whether the genre was a moral one or not, for it was thought that the idea of literature for entertainment did not really exist in the Middle Ages. Medieval literature, of course, was allowed some entertainment value by earlier scholars, but it was also required to instruct at the same time (*prodesse et delectare*, 'to instruct and delight' is a common phrase in medieval poetics). Not all critics now accept this dictum. After all, the moral, if there is one, of *Dame Sirith* and *De Clerico et Puella*, is not only cynical, but meagre and rather banal. Like a good deal of medieval literature, however, these two pieces are still worth reading simply because they are good stories well told.

REFERENCES

(in addition to those given in J.A.W. Bennett and G.V. Smithers, eds., *Early Middle English Verse and Prose*, Oxford: O.U.P., 2nd ed., 1968. (1st ed., 1966.)

Bédier, J (1894). *Les Fabliaux*. Paris: Champion. (6th ed., 1969.)
Nykrog, P. (1957). *Les Fabliaux*. Geneva: Droz.
Rychner, J. (1960). *Contribution à l'étude des fabliaux*. 2 vols. Geneva: Droz.
Muscatine, C. (1986). *The Old French Fabliaux*. New Haven, Conn.: Yale U.P.
Busby, K. (1982). Conspicuous by its Absence: the English Fabliau. *Dutch Quarterly Review* 12. 30-41.
Duval, J., and R. Eichmann (tr.) (1982). *Cuckolds, Clerics, and Countrymen*. [Translations into English of a selection of Old French Fabliaux.] Fayetteville, Ark.: University of Arkansas Press.

THE FOX AND THE WOLF
A STUDY IN MEDIEVAL IRONY

WIM TIGGES
(University of Leiden)

After critical neglect for more than half a century, the tale of *The Fox and the Wolf* has more recently inspired several scholars to a renewed approach to its obvious merits; 'obvious' because as H. Bergner (1973: 268) has remarked, the tale is included in all the important anthologies of Middle English literature. Bergner was responding to two studies in which its satirical aspects are discussed: Bercovitch (1966) and Von Kreisler (1970). These three articles, the first to adopt an analytical rather than a contextual approach, form the basis of the present study. I do not intend, therefore, to summarize the early scholarship, which has been aptly presented by Bergner in particular[1] nor to rehearse the history of the treatment of the theme of *The Fox and the Wolf* (henceforth *FW*), which is most conveniently summed up by G.V. Smithers.[2] I shall present here a critical reading of the tale to show, without neglecting its thematic relationship with other medieval literature (most notably *branche* IV of the Old French *Roman de Renart*), that its merits lie mainly in its delicate sense of irony.

My interpretation depends on the assumption that *FW* is really a composite of several genres. Early scholars, such as McKnight (1908, 1913) and Ker (1969:92ff) have referred to the poem in fairly neutral terms as a beast-epic, emphasizing its relationship with the Renart-cycle. Von Kreisler and Bercovitch stress the satirical elements of *FW*. Bergner, like Smithers, emphasizes the close correspondence of the text to the genre of the beast-epic, after discussing the relationship between

---

[1] See especially his ample footnotes for a complete bibliography.

[2] In Bennett and Smithers (1968:65-67), preceding their edition of the text, from which all quotations from *FW* have been taken. (The translations following quotations are my own.) For a more extensive discussion of the tale in this light, see McKnight, 1913:xliii-lxi, and also McKnight, 1908:497-509.

the tale and some well-defined genres such as the fable, the fabliau and the mock-heroic or mock-romantic parody. Although Bergner (1973:276-79) acknowledges the presence of fabulistic and (mock-)epic elements, he clearly states that *FW* can hardly be styled epic.

In my opinion *FW* is a satire which incorporates the genre of the beast-epic, as it does those of fable, epic, and, to a lesser extent, several other prominent medieval genres such as the fabliau and even religious allegory. These several aspects ironically illuminate one another, thereby enhancing the total meaning of the poem, making it something more ambitious than a mere light-hearted animal tale. As the interplay is primarily between the widely divergent themes of epic and fable, I shall introduce my reading of *FW* with a brief discussion of these genres as they feature in it. Allusions to other genres will be mentioned as they emerge in my analysis of the text.

When *FW* is called a beast-epic it is drawn into the traditional nomenclature of the Renart-cycle, so that the term 'epic' mainly serves to link the tale to the *Roman de Renart*[3] (henceforth *RR*), which has perhaps been best described as "a loose-knit series of tales by various hands" (Cohen, 1963:34). In the comparison with *FW* we are concerned only with its *branche* IV, a 478-line episode which is introduced by its author as a *"branche"*, and furthermore as a single jest or little joke (*un sol gabet*, l.19). He contrasts it with a sermon and a saint's life (ll.4-5), and continues *C'est de Renart, bien le savez, / Et bien oï dire l'avez* (ll.21-22). It is clear that the poet of this *branche* considers it to be merely an addition to an existing, supposedly well-known narrative: 'This is about Renard, you know him well, and have surely heard talk about him'. It is only in the opening lines of *branche* II (the oldest *branche* of the cycle) that there is any discussion of the work in terms of classical epic and its medieval equivalent; this episode is compared to that between *deus barons* (l.14). Moreover, a comparison is drawn between *RR* II and the *Iliad* (l.3). We can see that there is a contrast between the authorial presentation of *branches* II and IV of *RR*.

A similar contrast is found within the small compass of *FW*. In the opening line we read: *A vox gon out of þe wode go* ('a fox came out of the wood'), and later on, when the fox is already in the well and starts howling, *þer com a wolf gon ...* ('there came a wolf', l.108). The pro-

---

[3] Quotations from the Roman de Renart are from Martin (1882-87).

tagonists, then, are introduced in the same fashion as the animals in a fable, where the main characteristic of the animals is that they are types, not individuals as in the beast-epic. No doubt the first line of *FW*, the line that would catch the attention of the medieval (as of the modern) audience or reader, would suggest a fable rather than any other genre. It is only later in the tale that identification of the protagonists takes place, resulting in the individualization of character, and also (at least to those members of the medieval audience who were familiar with the French—or Flemish—*Renart*), providing a link with the Renart-cycle. Thus, the cock is almost immediately identified as *Sire Chauntecler* (1.37). In line 128 the fox guesses *Ich wene hit is Sigrim þat Ich here* ('I think I can hear Sigrim'), and he discloses himself as *Reneuard, þi frend* ('Renard, your friend, 1.133).

The author of *FW* has, then, implicitly 'mixed' his genres of fable and beast-epic, just as in *RR* we find a similar discrepancy between *chanson de geste* and *gabet*; but whereas in the latter text this mixture of genre occurs in different *branches*, which may well have been composed by different authors, in *FW* there is only one coherent tale, in which the protagonists are first presented as fable types, and subsequently as individualized characters. The contrast between the presentation of *FW* and its corresponding *branche* of *RR* has been noticed by Bergner (1973:270), but its importance, it seems, has been overlooked.

The English poet's mode of presenting his characters has several effects. For one thing, it shows that, although the author was basing his story on the Renart-cycle, he did not assume any great familiarity with this cycle, a fact that tallies with the few remains of Renart-poetry in medieval England. In spite of the numerous occurrences of more or less anthropomorphous foxes in medieval English art, the English of the period do not seem to have been very familiar with Renart in his literary shape.[4]

---

[4] Cf. Varty, 1967. In this book Varty adduces the evidence of 292 different artefacts based on the fox-theme as proof of his theory that "Reynard was much better known in England than extant literary evidence suggests" (p.24). Cf. also Wilson, 1952:136, which is referred to by Varty in a footnote to the above quotation. Bergner (1973: section IV, esp. 283) opposes these theories. A counter-argument that might be used here is that the MSS of very popular works may have been literally 'read to pieces'. At any rate, Bergner's statements about the absence of any assumption of popularity of the subject-matter in FW, especially in Chaucer's *Nun's Priest's Tale* and Caxton's translation of the Flemish *Reinaerde* seem to be convincing enough.

More important for our analysis of the tale in the light of its use of
irony, however, is the impact which the gradual change-over from the
fabulous to the epic mode must have made on the audience or the reader.
This type of 'abuse' of genre is to be regarded as a satirical device rather
than as a sign of decadence or a mishandling or misunderstanding, on the
part of the author, of this theme (see, for example, Heiserman, 1961).
The poet, seemingly presenting the unsuspecting reader with a fable,
suddenly transforms his types into characters, characters which, as will
be shown, assume an epic stature. For, after the identification of
Chauntecler in 1.37, the author prepares us for the disclosing of the name
of the protagonist or hero of the tale, Reneuard, by mere implication.
The delayed disclosure thereby obtains the effect of an epic 'identification
scene', as when Ulysses finally discloses his identity, of which the reader
has been aware all along, to the Phaeacians, thereby introducing an epic
element of dramatic irony.

The importance of the word *afingret* ('hungry') in 1.2, repeated in
1.4, has been stressed by Bergner (1973:270 and footnote): it indicates the
theme, which is hunger, but a hunger associated with *wo*. Perhaps
Bergner has over-emphasized, in connection with these opening lines, the
element of greed as *Leitmotiv*. Surely, at this stage at least the fox's
hunger is natural animal appetite rather than unnatural greed such as that
of the wolf. Anyway, the fox, like the wolf later on, is prepared to leave
his natural habitat, the wood, and to venture into the world of man, represented by the friary. The author wittily expands the fox's concern about
avoiding contact with men into an even greater concern about avoiding
women, which is entirely irrelevant within the context. The joke, of
course, is against women in the true medieval anti-feminist tradition, but
the comparison between hens and women suggests, ironically, that to the
fox meeting a single hen is the next worse thing to meeting fifty women;
it might well be, but in a different sense: Reneuard would prefer to meet
half a hundred hens, or at least the five that make up Chauntecler's little
harem.

From what follows in the poem it is clear that although the author
pretends ironically that the fox is going where his nose leads him,
Reneuard really knows where he is going: he recognizes the cloister wall,
looks around carefully, approaches the wall and leaps in through the first
breach he encounters. Although the wall has fallen down in places *som*
þerof wes afalle / And wes þe wal oueral tobroke ('part of it had fallen

down, and everywhere the wall was broken', ll.18-19), the gate of this neglected friary is locked (1.20). The order in which we are informed of the state of the cloister walls makes this passage ironic. A statement to the effect that the gate was locked, but that there were holes in the wall, would have spoiled the irony which is now upheld by the fact that the two statements are juxtaposed without any further comment. In any case, the situation is quite different in *RR* IV, where the fox has to run around and around the strong and high wall, until he finally manages to squeeze himself through a gap in the front porch (*RR* IV, ll.69-106).

The fox's laugh (1.23) seems to be one of scorn for the negligent hedge-keeper and bailiff at least as much as in exultation at the easy success of his raid so far: the human garden, supposed to be securely walled and protected, seems to have run wild.

Ironical, once again, therefore, is the fact that it is not a human being, but the cock who is the guardian of the hen-roost. The whole episode (ll.27-64) that contains the dialogue between the fox and the cock has been decried, and even called "out of proportion", especially as it seems to show some "inartistic cutting" (Wilson, 1968:248). However, it contains essential material providing links and parallels with later events in the story. A 'cutting' must of course be assumed if one reads *FW* in close connection with *RR* IV, where the fox's killing of three hens is related. But in *FW* the episode in which the fox carries the third hen along to the well, and in some versions of the story even uses it as a bait for the conviction of the wolf, does not occur. What is supposed to take place between ll.30 and 31 (Reneuard's killing and eating two of the hens) can indeed be read 'between the lines' in the ensuing debate, in which the fox answers Chauntecler's worried question: *Wat dest þou þare?* by informing him that he has only been practising a surgical operation. The effect of the absence of a factual statement about Reneuard's seizing, killing and eating of the hens is that the emphasis on the verbal battle between fox and cock is all the more prominent. In fact, the importance of dialogue, in *FW* in general, and in this part of it in particular, has been stressed by Bergner, who also emphasizes the reduction of realistic detail in comparison with *RR* IV, in favour of the 'inner realism' of the dialogue (1973:271, 273). Here, comparison with *The Nun's Priest's Tale* comes to mind, where rhetoric represents the art of persuasion *in optima forma*, and the episode with Chauntecler is therefore relevant, since it shows Reneuard's failure in this art, just as the Sigrim episode shows his success.

Besides, the Chauntecler scene shows Reneuard in his role as physician, again a traditional role, possibly the oldest of the beast-epic cycle.[5] The last line of his speech to the cock, *O þer sone axe after þe prest* ('or else you must at once fetch a priest', 1.52) ironically points forward to the role that Reneuard will presently play, and with more success. The cock, however, is not taken in.[6] Yet, in his speech his powerlessness to punish the fox physically is emphasized (*were I adoun, Ich mi ʒte, weste hit, he wolde* in ll.57-61 are all subjunctives). Once again, the impotence of the human element in this beast tale, the inability of man to interfere, is alluded to as well. The angrily alliterative 1.62, *mid pikes and stones and staues stronge* ('with pikes and stones and heavy sticks'), is not only an idle, and therefore ironical, threat, it also ironically foreshadows 1.284: *mid pikes and staues and ston--*, where the threat has now been turned into reality; only in the end it is the wolf who receives the punishment, whereas the cock has suggested it as fit for the fox (see also Von Kreisler, 1970:656-57).

Apparently, Reneuard does not expect the cock's straightforward reaction to his ironical speech; in any case, it strikes the fox completely dumb (1.65), and he will have to look elsewhere for his comfort. To account for his thirst a killing of some hens during his visit to the roost seems to be plausible, but again the author does not care to go into detail here. The fox, who does not seem to be aware of the existence of the well near-by (*Oueral he ede and sohvte*, 'he went and sought everywhere', 1.69), is yet said to be brought there by *his wiit* ('his intelligence'). This phrase, following *on auenture* ('accidentally') in the same line (1.70), must therefore be ironical. After this failure to deceive Chauntecler we are beginning to wonder how wise, or how stupid, this fox really is. This is stressed by the fox's being repeatedly reported to be non-plussed by the *ginne* of the buckets, a word that is used five times in this episode (ll.72, 77, 86, 103 and 125). The fox's lack of understanding is ironically underlined by the simple explanation on the part of the author:

---

[5] Cf. *Ecbasis Captivi* (ca. 940), Nivardus' *Isengrimus* (ca. 1149), and *RR* IV.

[6] Another traditional feature; cf. the Sprotinus episode in *Isengrimus*, and *The Nun's Priest's Tale*. The fox outwitted by the cock is another fable-motif: cf. Marie de France, *Fables*, No. 60: *Del cok e del gupil.*

Þat wes imaked mid grete ginne.
Tuo boketes þer he founde:
Þat oþer wende to þe grounde,
Þat wen me shulde þat on opwinde
Þat oþer wolde adoun winde

(ll.72-76)

(Which was built with great ingenuity. Two buckets he found there: one of
them went to the bottom, in such a way that when one wound up one, the other
would go down.)

... *grete ginne* indeed!

The author now proceeds to taunt his hero with his lack of understanding of simple mechanics. Lines 77-95 are a slow but steady exposure
of an almost predestined downfall (*Adoun he moste, he wes þerinne*—,
'he had to go down, as he was 'in for it", l.85); the fox has, as it were,
pressed the fatal button, he has put into motion (a downward motion) the
swikele ginne that will later on become the instrument of his own treach-
ery towards the wolf. Perhaps also the *swikele ginne* ('treacherous
device') serves as a parody of the epic machinery; the literal 'machinery'
certainly has a mysterious superiority, a super-animal (because human)
quality, with which neither fox nor wolf should really meddle.

In a speech full of proverbial cliché (ll.96-106) the fox now
indulges in self-pity rather than self-accusation. Again one senses the
parody, this time of the epic hero's self-condemnatory speech when he
feels he has let his fellows down. Yet, like a true Ulysses or Aeneas,
Reneuard steels himself against his misfortune when the wolf is brought
on stage. Like the fox, he has ventured *Out of þe depe wode* (l.109).[7] The
meeting of heroes will now soon take place, and after this the great battle,
which is one of words (Bergner, 1973:278). But first there is the
identification scene. The wolf, who is said to have immediately recognized the fox by his voice (ll.114-16), still asks, *pro forma* as it were,
who it is down there, and adds irony by asking: *Hertou Cristine oþer mi
fere?* ('Are you a Christian or my friend?', l.120). The second irony (the
first is that of the feigned non-recognition) is, however, directed at the

---

[7] Incidentally, the phrase *out of þe (...) wode* is the only reminiscence in *FW* of the
Isengrimus: egrediens silua mane Ysengrimus (l.1).

wolf himself: anyone who is his friend cannot be a Christian. A third level of irony can be adduced if the line is regarded as foreshadowing the fox's impersonating of the Christian *par example*, the priest.[8] The wolf's exhortation to the fox to *gabbe* [him] *nout* ('do not deceive him'), which is exactly what Reneuard is going to do, is another example of dramatic irony.

With the fox's recognition of his *kun* his *wiit* returns (ll.123-24). The word *ginne* is used for the trick that is going to bring the wolf down and the fox up. But the latter needs time, and therefore the recognition scene is prolonged. 'Aren't you Sigrim?' 'Yes indeed, but who are you?' 'I'll tell you, no lies: I am Reneuard, your friend' (ll.127-33). The very first apposition to Reneuard's proper name is a lie: Reneuard is neither Sigrim's 'kinsman' nor his 'friend', as will soon appear. By introducing the word *ibede* in l.135 the fox is gradually entering upon his role as a (mock)-priest. Ironically, his self-accusation in ll.96-106 had already placed him in the light of one who is about to enter upon a holy life (see Bercovitch, 1966:290-91), and the parody of religious instruction, which the fox significantly starts in l.139 with the remark *þou art ounwiis!* ('you are stupid!') culminates in a fine example of the unctuous hypocrisy of friardom in ll.158-66.

The doubtful wolf, wondering what *he* should do in the well, is told by the fox that *Her is þe blisse of Paradiis* ('here is the bliss of Paradise', l.140). At this stage the fox is not yet suggesting that he actually *is* in paradise, but that the well is *like* paradise—he is obviously 'thinking aloud'. His first, vague description of the food and drink to be found in good abundance at the bottom of what seems to be an ordinary well merely makes the wolf laugh (l.148). He, too, takes the fox's words as ironical: 'Come off it—if that's true you must be dead—'. No reply. Beginning to wonder whether the fox can really be dead, it is now the wolf who is thinking aloud: 'I saw you and your family not three days ago!' But was not three days the time it took for Christ to die, to descend into Hell and rise again? The collective dinner at the wolf's becomes suddenly reminiscent of the Last Supper, and the fox prepares himself and us for his Resurrection by associating himself with Christ in l.159. The dense wolf, of course, is unaware of the fact that in this little allegory the well stands for

---

[8] Perhaps it should also be borne in mind that traditionally the *wolf* is often referred to (in *Isengrimus* and in *RR*) as a monk or even an abbot.

Hell, not Paradise, nor does he recognize in the fox's further specification of the *mete* of 1.143 into *shep and get* (1.167) an allusion to the last Judgment. By now, further religious and allegorical allusions, such as that to the well of Jacob (see Bercovitch,1966:290), and also the immediate link a medieval audience would establish between a pit and the entrance to hell, have given an extra ironical framework to the dialogue. But the development of the plot turns vitally at 1.170. The sheep and goats remind the wolf, not of these Christian allusions to virtue and vice, good and evil, but of his own insatiable hunger. He is now morally blinded and ready to follow any instructions the fox may give. When the wolf mentions forgiving the fox's crimes against him, the latter immediately takes him up on this idea, reversing the procedure: the wolf shall 'confess' to the fox and be absolved by him. Reneuard can even afford to refuse shrift to the wolf at first, Sigrim is so willing: *Ich wot, toniȝt Ich worþe ded, / Bote þou do me somne reed* ('I am sure I shall die this night unless you give me some advice', ll.191-92). Again, this is dramatic irony, because the fox's counsel will almost be the death of the wolf.

The confession scene (ll.199-228) is one of the most complex passages in the whole poem. The wolf now reveals himself in his full stupidity and appears much as the self-confessing Vice of later drama, as a braggart, and as a pretended hero, the first by his phrase *Ich habbe ben qued al mi lif-daie* ('I have been wicked all my life', 1.200), the last by the next line *ich habbe widewene kors--* ('I have the curse of widows'): the widows' curse, apart from its biblical overtone, is reminiscent of the epic formula in which a battle is reported to be the cause of grief of the widows of the slain. Sigrim has killed a thousand sheep, he boasts (1.203), and the widows, one presumes, are the ewes. In reality, perhaps, the widows are the unfortunate owners of the sheep stolen by the wolf, the likes of the *povre wydwe* in Chaucer's *Nun's Priest's Tale*.

In all likelihood, however, the wolf has not *abiten* his *þousent shep* at one go, as an epic hero would kill his anonymous rabble-victims, but in the course of his life, and the figure is, of course, epic hyperbole anyway. One wonders whether the weight of the satirical attack is not here rather against the contemporary epic-romance than against the braggart-wolf. One remembers in this context the hyperbolic numbers said to be slain by Roland at his last stand: at first 20,000 against 400,000, the French are later sixty against 50,000, and Roland is repeatedly reported to attack his adversaries by the score.[9] Significantly, it is not the author as commentator, but Sigrim himself who exaggerates the number of his victims.

From Sigrim the braggart-hero we proceed to Sigrim the cuckold. Lines 211-20 seem to contain an allusion to Reneuard the courtly lover (cf. *RR* IV, 1.160, where Renart thinks he sees in the well Hermeline, *Sa famme qu'aime d'amor fine* ('his wife, whom he loves chivalrously'), a paradoxical statement in the light of the 'rules' of courtly love). The episode, of course, is a remnant of the reflection-in-the-water theme in *RR* IV. In the wolf's speech, the supreme irony is his remark that he thought, like everybody else, *that þat Ich iseie were so þ* ('what I saw should be true', 1.218), while he is actually looking down on Reneuard attempting to deceive him from the bottom of a well which he passes off as Paradise. What else remains to the fox but to forgive his dupe at *þisse nede* ('in this need', 1.225)? The wolf's reaction is typical: now that he is *in clene liue* ('in a way of life free from sin', 1.227) he no longer cares a straw for wife or children: a truly un-Christian point of view.

The fox now informs the wolf that the top-bucket is a *bruche of heuene blisse* ('an opening into the bliss of heaven', 1.233), and so it is indeed, but for the fox, not the wolf. The latter, with characteristic denseness, says: *þat is liȝt to done!* ('that is easy to do!', 1.236), when it is really his weight that is his literal downfall. Of course, the fox has realized that the wolf is heavier than he, and so he ascends while the wolf, half suspecting that there is something wrong here, comes down. Reneuard's farewell speech is nastily ironic. Still in his pretended role as a priest he promises to ring the wolf's death-knell (the clattering of the wolf's bucket on to the bottom?). A litotes and a nasty metaphor conclude this passage, and so we take our leave of the fox with the remark that he cared little about what happened to the wolf (1.260), an ironic remark seeing that the fox had previously taken upon himself the two roles of the physician, who is supposed to take care of the body, and the priest, who does the same for the soul.

Sigrim, however, is not yet through with his ordeal. The description of his state, *afringet so þat he ves wod* ('so hungry that he was mad (madly ravenous)', 1.285), has almost become formulaic. *Inou he cursede þat þider him broute* ('he often cursed the one who had brought him to

---

[9] Cf. also Brooke, 1969:158: "In the popular theology of the late eleventh and early twelfth centuries, ... the heathen were cattle for the slaughter."

that position', 1.259): if he is quite fair, it is himself he is cursing, not Reneuard.

Then, at last, the human world intervenes. It has seemed superfluous to discuss what has gone before in terms of anti-clerical satire, since this has been done by Bercovitch (1966) and Von Kreisler (1970). But the third part of the triptych which forms *FW*, the punishment of Sigrim (ll.261-95), has not been regarded in this light by previous students of this poem, though there is every reason for doing so. In this episode, Sigrim 'merely' receives his traditional corporal punishment (in *Isengrimus* he ultimately dies of his wounds), but the *sley* friars do not get away unscathed either. The neglect of their grounds has already been mentioned. Ironically, it is Ailmer the gardener, who would have been responsible for the upkeep of the garden walls (and therefore not 'less appropriately', as Smithers states in a note to 1.59 [Bennett and Smithers, 1968:300]), who, shirking his duty of singing matins, discovers Sigrim when he goes to the well to quench his thirst. He mistakes Sigrim for the devil, and this links the episode to the confession scene earlier on: much as Sigrim had taken the well to be the entrance to heavenly paradise, so the friars superstitiously mistake it for the exit of hell. Their 'reaction' to the appearance of the 'devil' is physical, rather than spiritual. The poem ends on a harsh note, with the friars beating and stabbing the wolf— without *for ʒeuenesse* (1.295), of which they are possibly incapable.[10] In their duping of Sigrim the 'real' friars are not much better than the false priest Reneuard.

As I have suggested earlier on, it is the combination of fable material and epic treatment that makes the beast-epic into a potential satire. In *FW*, the reader is presented with two traditional fables (the fox and the cock in the tree, the fox and the wolf in the well), upon which is superimposed the characterisation of the protagonists: the types of a cock, a fox and a wolf assume identities, and become the characters Chauntecler, Reneuard and Sigrim. In the 'ordinary' epic, the hero is a superhuman, usually national, character, who serves as an example, to which, however, we can never really hope to live up, although we are meant to. In the beast-epic, which is really a variety of the mock-epic, the hero is either a mock-hero or an anti-hero. Both variants are represented in *FW*. Reneuard, who is the 'hero' of the French cycle called after him, is an

---

[10] Cf. the emphasis on forgiveness in the confession scene (ll.175, 225).

anti-hero. He is admirable, but in an adverse way. He does not, I think, bear the brunt of the author's anti-clerical satire, as Bercovitch seems to suggest (1966:288), although part of the time he certainly stands for the corrupt cleric. But one of the relevancies of the Chauntecler episode is that it shows us Reneuard in another role, that of the physician, in the Middle Ages, as now, a ready object of satire. More importantly, *FW* shows us, in Reneuard's relation to the other two characters, that the success of the evil anti-hero is not entirely in his own hands, but is largely dependent on the quality of his antagonists.

Sigrim, the 'larger' of Reneuard's opponents, is far more than "the duped layman" (Bercovitch, 1966:288). He is even more than the "stupid, greedy, ever-hungry Wolf without whom the equally greedy but far more cunning Fox could not survive" (Von Kreisler, 1970:658). He is a mock-hero, a would-be epic hero like his predecessor Isengrimus in Nivardus' poem, or a would-be medieval nobleman as in the *Ecbasis Captivi*. Miserable failure is his eternal reward. Where Reneuard succeeds on his wanderings that even lead him down to a mock-epic Underworld, the well, Sigrim fails. That the quest is always one for food or drink rather than for a city to be founded or destroyed, or for a Holy Grail, only emphasizes the mockery inherent in the beast-epic.

Obviously, it is hard for us to identify with either of these 'heroes' (Bergner, (1973:276). Perhaps, therefore, the real hero of the tale is Chauntecler, whose claim has thus far been neglected. The disadvantage of this suggestion is that the cock is not really very heroic. He fails to protect his hens against the onslaught of the fox. He refuses to come down like a true hero and fight Reneuard, even against the odds. But then all fighting in *FW*, except the beating up of Sigrim by the friars, is verbal rather than physical. And in his verbal battle with Reneuard Chauntecler has the upper hand.

Perhaps we must see in *FW* an attempt on the part of a learned poet to decry the epic heroes in favour of the commonsensical point of view. Needless to say, this aspect of *FW* is subservient to the moral one that is inherent in the fable material in the tale. But by combining the two fables, adding the protagonists' identities, and placing the whole within a human framework, the author of *FW* has, like Chaucer in his *Nun's Priest's Tale*, done more than compose "merely a humorous beast-fable" (Tucker, 1908:109). He has presented his audience with an ironical satire in which to the simple plots of the two fables (traditionally dealing with the consequences of verbal trickery), are added the pretences of characters addicted to rhetoric: boasting heroes, hypocritical clerics and intellectual but ineffectual quacks. Thus, epic action is reduced to mock-epic action on the one hand (the entirely senseless descent of the two 'heroes' into the well), and to idle and immoral verbosity on the other (the dialogues). As has been shown, the poetic medium used to obtain the effect of verbal deceit that pervades FW, is bound up with its irony. Seemingly a mock-serious, even light-hearted animal tale, the poem is really a serious satire on human deceitfulness.

REFERENCES

Bennett, J.A.W., and G.V. Smithers (eds.) (1968). *Early Middle English Verse and Prose*. 2nd ed. Oxford: O.U.P. (1st ed., 1966).
Bercovitch, S. (1966). Clerical Satire in þe Vox and þe Wolf. *JEGP* 65. 287-94.
Bergner, H. (1973). *The Fox and the Wolf* und die Gattung des Tierepos in der mittelenglischen Literatur. *Germanisch-Romanische Monatschrift* 23. 268-85.
Brooke, C. (1969). *The Twelfth Century Renaissance*. London: Thames and Hudson.
Cohen, J.M. (1963). *A History of Werstern Literature*. Rev. ed. Chicago: Albine.
Heiserman, A.R. (1961). *Skelton and Satire*. Chicago: University of Chicago Press.
Ker, W.P. (1969). *Medieval English Literature*. Oxford: O.U.P. (1st publ. 1912)
Martin, E. (ed.) (1882-87). *Roman de Renart*. 3 Vols. Strasbourg.
McKnight, G.H. (1908). The Middle English Vox and Wolf. *PMLA* 23. 497-509.
McKnight, G.H. (ed.) (1913). *Middle English Humorous Tales in Verse*. Boston and London: D.C. Heath.
Tucker, S.M. (1908). *Verse Satire in England before the Renaissance*. Columbia University Studies in English. New York.
Varty, K. (1967). *Reynard the Fox: A Study of the Fox in Medieval Art*. Leicester: Leicester U.P.
Von Kreisler, N. (1970). Satire in *The Fox and the Wolf*. *JEGP* 69. 650-58.
Wilson, R.M. (1952). *The Lost Literature of Medieval England*. London: Methuen.
Wilson, R.M. (1968). *Early Middle English Literature*. 3rd ed. London: Methuen.

THE LAND OF COKAYGNE
SOPHISTICATED MIRTH

WIM TIGGES
(University of Leiden)

As is often the case with texts whose impact is mainly of a comical or mildly satirical nature, the Middle English "lay" of *The Land of Cokaygne* (henceforth *LC*) has been either neglected altogether or only mentioned in passing. It has received little critical attention. Early editors and critics concentrate on its Irish provenance, and on its relationship with the Old French *Fabliau de Cocagne* and the Middle Dutch *Dit is van dat edele Land van Cockaengen*.[1] The poem has been most convincingly referred to as a satire, a parody and a burlesque (see respectively Zesmer, 1961:186, Bennett and Smithers, 1968:137, and Blake, 1977:127), but it has also been noted to contain elements of a (goliardic) Utopia (see Pearsall, 1977:100, and especially Morton, (1978:15-25). This variety of interpretations seems to indicate a certain complexity of meaning. To the folk motif of the Delectable Land the poet has added a satirical element, which has led Kuczynski (1980:45-55) to the conclusion that the poem is both a Utopia and a satire. In the same article he also comments on the mixture of Celtic and Germanic material concerning a place which is untroubled by the vicissitudes of earthly life (1980:50-51), and comes to the conclusion that the poem was intended for a mixed audience. In this paper I intend to demonstrate that by collating a wide variety of traditions of the Delectable land and by adopting a sophisticated diction characteristic of courtly romance, the poet presents what is essentially a folk-tale, but informed with an ironic view of an essential element in human life: the desire for an escape to a never-never-land, no matter whether of supreme

---

[1] The OF analogue, and part of the MDu one, have been edited and discussed by Väänänen (1947). The two known versions of the MDu poem can be found in Priebsch (1894). The so-called Kildare poems, to which *LC* belongs, were first edited and discussed by Heuser (1904). For the history and affiliations of the folktale elements, see Poeschel (1878) and Bolte and Polivka (1918:iii.244ff).

materialism (abundant food, clothes and sex), asceticism (the monastery) or chivalry (the romantic pleasance).

One aspect of the poem's sophistication is the superimposition of at least nine variants of the Other World.[2] The traditions with which the poet seems to demonstrate familiarity are: 1 The folk tradition of the land of "Fair Ease", whose bliss consists in a superfluity of food and drink, separated from the outside world by an unpleasant, almost insurmountable obstacle. It is this tradition which links *LC* to the OF and MDu analogues. 2 The Earthly Paradise of Christian legend, with which Cokaygne is favourably compared. 3 The Celtic myth of the Blessed Isles, like those visited by St Brendan. 4 Related to this, the fabulous western islands described in the Old Irish travelogues or Immrama, describing the voyages of legendary travellers such as Bran, Mael Dúin and the Uí Chorra. 5 The parodies of these travelogues, as presented in *The Vision of MacConglinne*. It is the apparent acquaintance of the poet with the last three traditions that supports the theory that the poem is of Irish derivation, as argued in particular by Henry (1972:120-41). 6 The classical account of the Golden Age, as found in the first book of Ovid's *Metamorphoses* and in Virgil's Fourth Eclogue. 7 The medieval tradition of the *locus amoenus*, the enclosed pleasance of romance tradition. 8 The notion of the cloister as a paradise, which is discussed by Henry and especially by Hill (1975:55-56). It is this element in particular which creates a certain ambiguity in the possible interpretation of the poem, since the cloister could be regarded in this way from a favourable point of view: as an ideal, self-sufficient community, but also from the unfavourable point of view of the disappointed layman or the disillusioned cleric: as a self-centred and pleasure-loving society. 9 A possible reference to the Islamic paradise with its accommodating *houris* (see Metlitzki, 1977:210-19).[3]

It may well be the case, as Henry suggests (1972:134ff), that the author of *LC* was a Franciscan criticizing the all-too-worldly behaviour of Cistercian monks in a particular Irish cloister. However, the total ef-

---

[2] For my discussion of this topic I am greatly indebted to Patch (1950). See also Baring-Gould, 1977:89-91.

[3] In the light of the theory, never satisfactorily proved but not definitely rejected either, that most medieval humorous tales, especially those like the *fabliaux*, where the humour is connected with an erotic theme or plot, are ultimately derived from the East, the potential presence of an undercurrent of Eastern material should, I think, be taken into account. (Cf. Benfey, 1859.)

fect of the poem transcends such a limited reading. Therefore I shall en-
deavour to demonstrate how the poet satirizes the human desire for escape in general by means of a sophisticated, courtly diction, and, by doing
that, burlesques in passing the types of text, popular with a fairly general
audience, that accommodate this desire by a frequently facile indulgence
in wish-fulfilment: the romance, the fabliau, the travelogue, and even the
account of a delectable place after death.

The author of *LC* sets out to describe a land better than St Brendan's Island, better even than the Earthly Paradise: *þoʒ Paradis be miri
and briʒt,/ Cokaygn is of fairir siʒt* ('Although Paradise be delightful and
beautiful, Cokaygne is more beautiful to look upon', ll.5-6).[4] Instead of
enumerating the assets of Cokaygne, he now proceeds to decry those of
Eden (ll.7-16), but there does not seem to be so much difference after all:
as in Paradise, also in Cokaygne there are neither care nor labour (l.18),
no nightfall (l.26), no discord (l.27), no death (l.28), and no harmful
animals (l.31). But at this stage the poet begins to overdo things. From the
absence of serpent, wolf and fox, he proceeds to less obnoxious animals
one would not mind encountering in a land of bliss, unless one happens to
be a refined aristocrat, monk or otherwise, secluded in the ivory tower of
castle or cloister: horse, cow, sheep, swine, goat. Clearly the land of
Cokaygne is no pastoral world, nor is it a world in which animals provide
toil and trouble.

By the time we reach ll.37-38: *Nis þer flei, fle, no lowse/ In cloþ,
in toune, bed, no howse* ('There is neither fly, flea nor louse in clothing,
city, bed or house'), one begins to have doubts as to the poet's
noblemindedness; after a series of traditional, rhetorical negations (see,
for example, Patch, 1950:171, and Hill, 1975:57) a stage of bathos has
suddenly been reached. By his continuation, however, the poet suggests
that he is doing no more than simply denying the presence of any
unpleasant elements: nasty weather and blindness are as absent as the
muck which is the consequence of keeping cattle. This subtle shifting of
tone is a first indication of the mixture of genres the poet is employing all
through the poem. At one level he is repeating the topic of the "seven joys
of heaven" with its obverse catalogue, at another he is parodying this very
idea by giving it a slightly absurd bias, and at a third he is pointing for-

---

[4] All quotations from *LC* have been taken from Bennett and Smithers, 1968:136-44.

ward to the folkloristic catalogue of ll.51-64, itself possibly a parody of
the romantic one of ll.65-100.

In the first 50 lines we find nothing that is really absurd. Of course,
the description of Cokaygne is entirely unrealistic, but then the land is a
kind of Earthly Paradise, only superior. The connection is made by the
mention of Paradise in l.5, by the allusions already mentioned, and also
by the reference to the four conventional characteristics of Earthly Paradise, the four rivers, the soft climate, the fruitful soil and its being the
dwelling place of Enoch and Elias.

But, while the *riuers gret and fine/ Of oile, melk, honi, and wine*
(ll.44-45) can be easily accepted as metaphors of natural or rather super-
natural opulence, abbey walls made of pasties (l.54) defy such a reading.
With the opening of the second section (ll.51-100) the author has definitely turned to folkloristic Cokaygne imagery, that of buildings made of
food, and we may now see retrospectively that the rivers were meant to
anticipate this, and that their contents have to be taken literally. What is
particularly interesting is that the food imagery is much less prominent
than in the OF analogue, and further that it is associated with a monastery.[5] It is at this stage, too, that the satire begins, since the poem
clearly suggests that the white and grey monks, of whatever order they
be, are living in a kind of cloud-cuckoo-land.

To a layman, this must have been a recognizable picture of any
monastery, to judge by the multifarious examples of anti- monastic criticism of the later Middle Ages. The monastery was a kind of island in
society, secluded from the surrounding world by its walls, "ideally a
replica of heaven on earth" (Southern, 1970:230), and in any case a veri-
table *paradisus claustralis* (Hill, 1975:56). Particularly interesting, in the
light of the mention made of the four rivers in l.45 of *LC*, the spices
(ll.73-78) and the roses and lilies (ll.79-80), is the description by Peter
Damien in addressing Abbot Hugh of Cluny: "I saw a *Paradise* ... watered
by the *four streams* of the Gospels, overflowing with spiritual virtues. I
saw a garden bringing forth all kinds of delicious *roses and lilies*, heavy
with the sweet fragrance of scents and *spices*, ... (Southern, 1970:230,
italics mine).

---

[5] For a discussion of the identity of the white and grey monks of l.52, see note to
l.164 in Bennett and Smithers, 1968:341. For an interesting discussion of "white
canons" (the Premonstratensians) and their double monasteries, see Heer, 1974:60.

We can also see a link between the cloister as the "gate of Paradise" (Heer, 1974:56) or even Paradise itself, and the excessive consumption of food by monks. On the latter aspect Heer informs us that "From very primitive times honouring the dead has taken the form of ceremonious eating and drinking" (1974:52) and so we are led to assume that "The complaints about the intemperate eating and drinking among monks and collegiate clergy, which in the twelfth century became increasingly strident (...) must be seen in this context" (1974:52-53). Of course, what comes to mind here is the Irish tradition of the "Wake".

In *LC*, the monastery is a mixture of the "traditional" Cokaygne (ll.54-66) and of the *locus amoenus* of medieval romance, which abounds in precious stones (ll.67-70, 88-94), exotic spices (ll.71-78), the traditional roses and lilies (ll.79-82), the medicinal fountain (ll.83-87) and bird-song (ll.95-100). The whole section, which is purely descriptive, reads like a parody of similar episodes in romances, an exaggeration of the rhetorical device of the catalogue. From the "vulgar" catalogue of puddings and pies the poet shifts almost imperceptibly to the aristocratic one of gems and ginger: even the food-list is not quite so common as the title of the poem would suggest. Far from describing the everyday fare of the common man, or the frugal diet of the monastery, the poet enumerates the items on an aristocratic *menu*, a fact which, together with the sophisticated vocabulary in which this section is couched, points to a type of audience which was all too familiar with the courtly way of life.[6]

Just when this audience imagines it has left the land of Readymade and finds itself on familiar ground in the romantic pleasance, the author once again takes up the food imagery. This time the audience is asked to believe that roasted geese fly into the abbey, announcing themselves with what was no doubt a familiar street-cry, or rather, a subtle variation of one: *Gees, al hote, al hot!* (1.104). These geese, and their equally obliging colleagues the larks (1.107) were no doubt suggested by the previous catalogue of the pleasance birds; the numerous singing birds, several of which are mentioned in ll.96-97, are contrasted to the cooking birds of ll.102-10. Likewise the *gilofre* ('clove') and *canel* ('cinnamon') with which they season themselves (1.110) are ready to hand in the pleasance (cf. ll.76-77).

---

[6] The number of French-derived words in *LC* is surprisingly high,being around 10.5 % of the total lexis. There are 24 words in *LC* which the *OED* gives as first recorded in this text. Many of these are from the fields of cooking and the lapidary.

In the next episode (ll.113-46) the monks' style of living is recounted. It proves to be that of the courtly romantic lover. The poet emphasizes that the monks are young (l.121), and they are so *hei3 of mode* ('high-spirited', l.125) that they actually take off from the ground and fly. Their sleeves and hoods remind not only the abbot of real birds—no doubt the author is touching upon a familiar sight: these monks are wearing the fashionable wide-sleeved tunics. The whole passage is very reminiscent of Chaucer's description of the Squire in the General Prologue to *The Canterbury Tales*.(Robinson, 1957:ll.79-100). The squire, too, is young (l. 79), his tunic has *sleves longe and wyde* (l.93) and he is even compared to a bird (ll.91, 98). The common source of both passages is presumably the *Roman de la Rose*, where the ideal young lover is extensively described (Lecoy, 1970:ll.2075-2220).

In the description of the abbot's futile attempt to get his underlings back to earth (ll.133-46) the courtly atmosphere is somewhat debunked. The whole scene is remarkably reminiscent of savages beating and dancing around war-drums, and may be compared in its presentation to the garbled accounts in the romance of *Kyng Alisaunder* or in *Mandeville's Travels*. Henry (1972:136) connects this scene with the *pulsatio tabule* to waken monks in the morning. The flying, I think, is meant to allude to the fact that these monks not only offend against the vows of poverty, chastity and obedience (cf. Hill, 1975:55) but also against that of stability of place.

In fact, the monks' doings as described in this passage are as much subject to daily regulation as ordinary monastic life: first they say mass (they are not entirely idle in their religious observance, although they seem to skip the inconveniently early lauds and matins), next they take to their flying games, which take the place of the manual or intellectual labour required of real-life monks (cf. Hill, 1975:57-58). The exuberant dancing around the *maidin* ('girl') also seems to have the marks of a regular habit, and so off to their *collacione* ('light evening meal').

The fourth section of *LC* (ll.147-82) begins by describing the nunnery. The nuns, too, are young (l.152), and the river of sweet milk (l.149) seems the most appropriate of the four streams mentioned in ll.45-46 for the nunnery to be situated on. Initially, the sweet milk, the boating, and the naked swimming seem to emphasize their innocence (or chastity: Hill, 1975:58). But the young monks are there to "instruct" them (l.165). The account of the goings-on between the nuns and the monks takes us back once more to folkloristic Cokaygne, where not only food

and drink, but also abundant sex is an important asset, as in the OF analogue. As is usual in medieval texts of the nature of a fabliau, the act of
intercourse is euphemistically paraphrased, in this case in terms of prayer
(*oreisun*, 1.165) and dancing (*iambleue*, 1.166), thereby emphasizing not
only the oral and genital aspects of physical love, but also once again the
clerical and courtly aspects.

To some extent the episode is in accordance with the criticism that
might be incurred by the institution of the double monastery, once a
characteristic feature of Irish monasticism and partially revived in England during the twelfth century (Heer, 1974:60). Once more, anti-
monastic satire is presented. The absence of even the mildest anti-feminist
satire may be attributed to the chivalric outlook of the poet.

Having concluded his description of Cokaygne by alluding to
another folkloristic feature, also found in the OF analogue, that excessive
sleep as culmination of laziness is rewarded (ll.173-77), the poet ends on
a note which seems to be as (mildly) defensive of monastic life as the preceding episodes have been (mildly) satirical of it. The seven years'
penance is comparable to the traditional mountain of rice pudding in the
later Dutch analogue of *Luilekkerland*, first recorded in 1546. In general, it stands for the near-insurmountable obstacle that protects these
delectable places against easy and frequent visitation from outside. More
specifically, the passage (ll.177-82) leads us back to the world of religion
which sets the tone of the poem. Translated into religious precepts, the
symbols of Cokaygne and the swine's dung teach us that we must accept a
life of hardship and overcome obstacles on our path before we can enter
the abode of heavenly bliss. In terms of common psychology the meaning
of these symbols is that in order to lead a balanced life one must take the
rough with the smooth, a common enough precept, but seldom presented
in such an original way.

Even in relation to monastic life the seven years' wading in swine's
dung makes sense: it may stand for the period of tedious study during the
novitiate, or perhaps more generally for the material hardship that
monastic life entailed. In his final prayer, the author makes it clear that
the unpleasant side of life can be seen as a penance. He also seems to imply
that the good life he has so exuberantly described can be experienced in
this world (ll.184-85). On the other hand, the very absurdity of the
nature of the "penance" finally shows up the impossibility of ever being

able to escape towards the Delectable Land—unless one inhabits it already, by belonging to the secular or clerical aristocracy.

REFERENCES

Baring-Gould, S. (1977). *Curious Myths of the Middle Ages*. London: Jupiter Books. (1st publ., 1866.)
Benfey, T. (1859). *Pantschatantra*. Leipzig.
Bennett, J.A.W. and G.V. Smithers (eds.) (1968). *Early Middle English Verse and Prose*. 2nd ed. Oxford: O.U.P. (1st ed., 1966)
Blake, N. (1977). *The English Language in Medieval Literature*. London: Methuen.
Bolte, J. and G. Polivka (1918). *Anmerkungen zu den Kinder- und Hausmärchen der Brüder Grimm*. Leipzig.
Heer, F. (1974). *The Medieval World. Europe 1100-1350*. Transl. J. Sondheimer. London: Sphere Books. (1st publ., 1962.)
Henry, P.L. (1972). The Land of Cokaygne: Cultures in Contact in Medieval Ireland. *Studia Hibernica* 12. 120-41.
Heuser, W. (1904). *Die Kildare-Gedichte*. Bonn: Hanstein [Bonner Beiträge zur Anglistik 14]. 1904. (Repr. Darmstadt, 1965.)
Hill, T.D. (1975). Parody and Theme in the Middle English "Land of Cokaygne". *Notes and Queries* 220. 55-59.
Kuczynski, P. (1980). Utopie und Satire in *The Land of Cokaygne. Zeitschrift für Anglistik und Amerikanistik* 28. 45-55.
Lecoy, F. (ed.) (1970). *Roman de la Rose*. Paris: Champion.
Metlitzki, D. (1977). The Muslim Paradise as the Land of Cokaygne. In: *The Matter of Araby in Medieval England*. New Haven and London: Yale U.P. 210-19.
Morton, A.L. (1978). *The English Utopia*. London: Lawrence and Wishart. (1st publ., 1952.)
Patch, H.R. (1950). *The Other World According to Descriptions in Medieval Literature*. Smith College Studies in Modern Languages. New Series. Cambridge, Mass.
Pearsall, D. (1977). *Old and Middle English Poetry*. London: Routledge and Kegan Paul.
Poeschel, J. (1878). Das Märchen vom Schlaraffenlande. *Beiträge zur Geschichte der deutschen Sprache und Literatur* 5. 389-427.
Priebsch, R. (1894). Noch einmal 'Van dat edele lant van Cockaengen'. *Tijdschrift voor Nederlandse Taal- en Letterkunde* 13. 185-91.
Robinson, F.N. (ed.) (1958). *The Works of Geoffrey Chaucer*. 2nd ed. London: O.U.P. (1st ed., 1933.)
Southern, R.W. (1970). *Western Society and the Church in the Middle Ages*. Harmondsworth: Penguin Books.
Väänänen, V. (1947). Le fabliau de Cocagne. *Neuphilologische Mitteilungen* 48. 3-36.
Zesmer, D.M. (1961). *Guide to English Literature. From Beowulf through Chaucer and Medieval Drama*. New York: Barnes and Noble.